The Standard of Living

The Standard of Living

The Tanner Lectures
Clare Hall, Cambridge, 1985

AMARTYA SEN

and
John Muellbauer, Ravi Kanbur
Keith Hart, Bernard Williams

edited by
Geoffrey Hawthorn

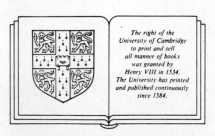

*The right of the
University of Cambridge
to print and sell
all manner of books
was granted by
Henry VIII in 1534.
The University has printed
and published continuously
since 1584.*

CAMBRIDGE UNIVERSITY PRESS

Cambridge
New York   Port Chester
Melbourne   Sydney

Published by the Press Syndicate of the University of Cambridge
The Pitt Building, Trumpington Street, Cambridge CB2 1RP
40 West 20th Street, New York, NY 10011, USA
10 Stamford Road, Oakleigh, Melbourne 3166, Australia

First published 1987
First paperback edition 1988
Reprinted 1990

Printed in Great Britain at the University Press, Cambridge

British Library cataloguing in publication data

The Standard of living: the Tanner
lectures, Clare Hall, Cambridge, 1985.
1. Cost and standard of living
I. Sen, Amartya   II. Hawthorn, Geoffrey
339.4'7   HD6978

Library of Congress cataloguing in publication data

The Standard of living
(The Tanner lectures)
Bibliography.
1. Cost and standard of living.   2. Basic needs.
3. Quality of life.   I. Sen, Amartya Kumar.
II. Hawthorn, Geoffrey.   III. Series.
HD6978.S73   1986   339.4'7   86-18832

ISBN 0 521 32101 8 hardback
ISBN 0 521 36840 5 paperback

Contents

269430 3

Contributors

AMARTYA SEN is Lamont University Professor at Harvard University.

JOHN MUELLBAUER is an Official Fellow of Nuffield College, Oxford.

RAVI KANBUR is Professor of Economics at the University of Essex.

KEITH HART is an Assistant Lecturer in Social Anthropology at Cambridge University and currently Visiting Professor at the University of the West Indies, Jamaica.

BERNARD WILLIAMS is Provost of King's College, Cambridge.

GEOFFREY HAWTHORN is Reader in Sociology and Politics at Cambridge University and a Fellow of Clare Hall.

Introduction

The Tanner Lectures are the idea of Obert Clark Tanner, now Emeritus Professor of Philosophy at the University of Utah. They are intended in the Trustees' words 'to advance and reflect upon the scholarly and scientific learning relating to human values and valuations'; they were formally established at Clare Hall Cambridge on 1 July 1978, and are given annually at Harvard, Michigan, Stanford, Utah, Brasenose College Oxford and Clare Hall, and occasionally elsewhere.

It is part of the point of the lectures that they shall be published. This is done by the University Presses of Utah and Cambridge in volumes edited by Sterling McMurrin under the title *The Tanner Lectures on Human Values*. A shortened version of the two lectures given by Amartya Sen in Cambridge appears, with those given elsewhere in 1985, in Volume VII (McMurrin 1986). The fellows of Clare Hall have decided that the purpose of the lectures, for which they themselves are responsible, might be furthered by publishing them in full and by including in that publication some of the comments made at the subsequent seminar. The Tanner Trustees and the Syndics of the Cambridge University Press have agreed, and the present volume is the first result.

The 'standard of living' could not more directly have addressed Obert Tanner's intention. If not always under this description, it has become one of the first considerations of government; maintaining and improving it has become one of the central expectations of those who are governed. Indeed, in the extension almost everywhere of democracy, or at least, in the aspiration almost everywhere to democracy, in what is expected of modern states and of the economies over which these states more or less deliberately preside, and in the increasing concern with the condition of the developing countries since the 1950s, it may not be an exaggeration to say that, with national security and defence, it has become one of the two main objects of politics. But because it has as a result become such a highly charged issue, because of the difficulty of deciding what, exactly, it consists in, and because of the increasingly technical complexity of the answers to that question – all of which are themselves related to the complications of modern societies, the scope of modern states, and the increasing influence of economists in public policy – each advance in understanding how to think about it has been accompanied by further confusion and doubt. As so often in such matters, the more that seems to be known, the more that is said, and the more, practically, that is attempted, the less it seems that many, including many of those most closely involved, understand. Amartya Sen is an exception. He is as familiar with the historical project of his subject as he is with the variety of modern economies, as sensitive to the moral and political implications of economic analysis as he is expert and innovative in its techniques. He is accordingly, and almost uniquely, able to grasp, connect and convey the range of issues that arise in 'the standard of living'.

'The value of the living standard', as he puts it, 'lies in the living'. And if that means, against some prevailing academic fashions, that we have to reject being precisely wrong in favour of being vaguely right, so be it. But this is not to say that one can be cheerily – or in the popular conception of economists and what they do, even gloomily – loose. Much of what falls within 'the standard of living', like much of living itself, may not admit much empirical precision. And even if it did, such precision would usually have little point for those in government, who act with instruments that are blunt in conditions which they only fitfully control. Conceptual precision, however, is quite a different matter and is in this issue as important for citizens as it is for social scientists. It is Sen's first concern. In the first lecture, he criticises existing approaches to the standard of living in terms of utility and income and wealth, or 'opulence'. In the second, he makes a case for thinking of it in terms of human 'functionings' and 'capabilities'. In both, he shows that the argument consists in much more than tidying up a few loose ends. Three issues introduce the point. The first is one to which Sen refers only in passing in this volume; the second is still open at the end of it; the third remains implicit throughout.

The first is the confusion that can come from not observing the seemingly simple distinction between defining the standard of living and explaining it. The ease with which this can be done, and the muddle that can result, come out clearly in what is still perhaps the most sustained academic dispute about any actual standard of living, that in England in the years of the Industrial Revolution, between about 1750 and 1850. In their paper on 'the theoretical basis of pessimism' in this dispute, Hartwell and Engerman distinguish the three different questions in it (1975:193–4).[1] Did the standard of living of the working class rise in this period or not? Did it even fall? Would this class have been better off if there had been no industrialisation at all? And would they have been better off if industrialisation had occurred, but had taken a different course?

As von Tunzelmann says, having thus introduced some clarity into the matter, Hartwell and Engerman themselves proceed at once to confuse it: they suppose that the 'pessimists' are those who believe that the working class's standard of living fell, and who believe that the answer to the second question – the question of whether this class would have been better off if there had been no industrialisation at all – is 'yes' (von Tunzelmann 1985). In the first place, it is perfectly possible to answer 'yes' or 'no' to each of the three questions and be consistent. Even if one thinks that the standard of living did go up, one might also think that it would have gone up even faster without industrialisation, or if industrialisation had taken a different course. Conversely, it is perfectly possible to believe that the standard of living went down, and that it would have gone down even further if industrialisation had not occurred. (Most economic historians seem now at least to agree that real wages were fairly constant until about 1820, and rose thereafter.) As it happens – and apart from the wholly nostalgic, the Chestertons and Bellocs and others who have never seriously thought about the issue – the pessimists fall into three clear groups. One includes those like E. P. Thompson, who think that standards did fall, and that industrialisation would have brought more benefits if the ownership and control of capital had been in different hands, if it had in this or some similar (if undefined) respect been more 'socialist'. A second argues like the Hammonds, who were more agnostic about the course of the standard of living itself, but believed that industrialisation would have brought more benefits if the government had softened the consequences of enclosure, set a minimum wage for unskilled workers, and in enabling them to combine, allowed a fair wage for the skilled. A third includes von Tunzelmann himself, who argues that industrialisation would have brought more benefits and produced more growth if it had not been so capital-intensive.

But several of the pessimists, as Hartwell and Engerman see, have obscured their case by failing to separate the counterfactual question of whether the standard of living could have risen more, and more quickly, from the factual question of whether it rose at all. As Sen makes clear in his reply here to Keith Hart, not only are these questions distinct, but it is also the case that answering 'yes' to the counterfactual questions, for instance by showing that the productivity of labour could have been higher, does not necessarily give a similar answer to the more factual one. An affirmative answer to that would depend 'on the distribution of the aggregate supply and the utilisation of commodities in giving people the ability to do this or be that'. A recent contribution to the more purely factual question takes this point and suggests that instead of looking at estimates of income, which are possibly invalid, certainly unreliable, and difficult to interpret, one can look at trends in height (Floud and Wachter 1982; Floud 1984). This more exactly captures the distribution of commodities and, in concentrating on one of the effects that commodities have, suggests Sen's 'functionings', and hence 'capabilities'.

The second issue which makes the case for conceptual precision, and for the distinctions that Sen himself proposes, is that of what has often been referred to as the 'relativity' of living standards. This comes out clearly, and often very passionately, in arguments about poverty. In Sen (1983a), to which he refers to the end of the first lecture, and in his reply to Townsend's criticisms of that paper (Townsend 1985; Sen 1985c:161), Sen summarises his view in the remark that poverty – and by implication the standard of living more generally – 'is an absolute notion in the space of capabilities but very often it will take a relative form in the space of commodities or characteristics'. That is to say, there are certain capabilities – the capability remarked upon by Adam Smith, for instance, to appear in public without shame – which are absolute. If they are desirable at all, they are desirable for all. It is the resources or commodities that are needed to realise them, and not they themselves, which will vary through time and across space. In late eighteenth-century Glasgow, as Smith himself remarked, it may have been impossible to avoid shame without appearing in a linen shirt. In late twentieth-century London, as a respondent in a recent survey is reported as saying, it may be impossible to avoid it without being able to claim to give one's children treats.[2]

So much is clear and, perhaps, acceptable. What remains open, obviously difficult, perhaps indeterminate, but certainly crucial is, as Bernard Williams explains, the question of whether something like appearing in public without shame 'might be derived from some more basic capability', like that for self-respect, the question of whether such basic capabilities can usefully be thought of as rights, and the further, and perhaps more fundamental, question of whether, if such capabilities, perhaps 'absolute' capabilities, can be defined, their absoluteness lies in nature or in convention. The difficulty is, in a general way, familiar, but both Sen, in these lectures, and Williams, here and elsewhere (e.g., 1985:152–5), have set it out very clearly. An answer from nature will almost certainly underdetermine what, in any particular case, we may want to decide and do. Wholly non-conventional needs are very minimal things. Yet an answer from convention will be open to the objections that it is indeed *only* an answer from convention, that a convention cannot without further argument be taken to be its own defence – that, as Sen, Williams and John Muellbauer all point out, people may just have resigned themselves to it – and that defending it, or not, will in the end, in Williams' words, have thus to 'cycle back' (perhaps *via* comparisons with conventions elsewhere) to human nature, or real interests, or something of that sort. Yet the cycling-back may not be an entirely argumentative matter. 'The excellence or satisfactoriness of a life', as Williams has put it, 'does not stand to beliefs involved in that life as premise stands to conclusion.' An 'excellent life', even a satisfactory one, 'is characterised by having those beliefs, and most of the beliefs will not be about [the] agent's dispositions or life, or about other people's dispositions, but about the social world' (Williams 1985:154). The value of the living standard does indeed seem to lie in the living. The second argument in favour of conceptual precision is not to avoid that fact, but to try to see exactly what it might mean.

Nevertheless, living is inescapably collective, and no one can now believe that collective life, for instance in something called 'the market', takes a natural course. It is, even if only by default, directed. Modern governments may never be able to act precisely. But, however imprecisely they can actually do it, they do have to have a fairly precise sense of what it is that they might or might not be trying to do. This is the third reason for insisting on conceptual precision. Neither Sen nor any of his commentators deals directly with the questions that this raises. Sen's own first concern in these lectures is with distinguishing the idea of the standard from explanations of it, and then with the idea itself, not with what might be done about that standard in any particular place at any particular time. Moreover, as he says in reply to Ravi Kanbur, he is here in these two lectures less concerned with the question of aggregation, the question that has to be answered for public policy, than with the prior question of the standard itself for the individual.[3] But much of what he and his commentators have to say does bear upon what governments and other agencies might do.

Many governments and non-governmental agencies, for example, take some kind and degree of responsibility for what have come to be called the 'basic needs' of the poor. Sen shows that the foundations of such talk, the bases of the needs, have not been altogether clear. In addition, all governments have to consider the fact that most of the people for whom they might be making policy, whether these people are poor or not, live in households. These include children and, often, disadvantaged women. This raises questions of distribution and more technical questions of 'equivalence' – questions which are distinct from those of aggregation to the level of the 'social', or more exactly the public, good – to which Muellbauer and Hart in different ways address themselves. Moreover, governments and other agencies have to understand, and not just pre-emptively to decide, the extent to which households in the societies for which they are responsible can, in Hart's phrase, 'provision themselves', and the extent to which provision has to come through some other institution or set of institutions. The interest of Hart's paper lies in the attention it draws to the often intricate and shifting connections that exist between 'self-provisioning' and provisioning by other means in three economies: those of grain farmers and herders in the West African savanna – the now stricken 'Sahel' – of textile workers in nineteenth-century Lancashire, and of industrial societies now. Such connections, as Hart and Sen in their different ways explain, make it dangerous to make inferences from estimates of income. And it is part of the main point of what Sen has to say, as he reaffirms in his reply to Muellbauer, that commodities – income itself, things which can be exchanged for income, and things which can be thought of as income – must be distinguished from what he calls 'functionings'. Functionings are 'features of the state of an existence of a person', not things which the person or the household can own or produce.

Moreover, as Sen says at the end of the second lecture, it is important, if not always easy, to distinguish functionings from capabilities to function and capabilities to choose to function. Capabilities imply freedoms. That is part of the point of considering them. Many people, and some governments, do pay attention to questions of freedom. Sen himself, as well as Kanbur and Muellbauer, explain what might be involved in giving this notion some practical clarity and operational sense, and what might be involved in comparing its *ex ante* attractions with its *ex post* results. But because a person's set of what Sen calls 'feasible functioning bundles' is also that person's capability, 'there is a simultaneous and two-way relationship between functionings and capabilities'. Some capabilities, of course, as Williams makes clear, may not relate to choice 'over the good that itself contributes to the increase in well-being or the standard of living' – it would be odd to claim that the capability of living longer, or of being taller, consists in being able to choose to die earlier or become smaller, and that this ability increases one's standard of living. And many capabilities – to buy yet another make of washing powder, for instance, as Williams says, in which to launder one's shirt – are trivial. But it does make conceptual as well as practical sense eventually to consider what he refers to as 'sets of co-realisable capabilities' and thus to think about the social and political conditions in which individuals might acquire such sets.

Nevertheless, questions of aggregation, let alone those of a more directly empirical and political kind, cannot be answered, cannot even indeed be asked, before the idea of the living standard itself is clear. Sen's merit is to have done much to make it so: as even his critics would have now to concede, to have made it a great deal clearer than it has previously been where the argument is and what it is about.

I am grateful for the help I received in arranging the occasion, and in preparing the results for publication, from others at the college, from Francis Brooke and Keith Lloyd at the Cambridge University Press, from the four commentators, and above all, and at a very difficult time for him, from Amartya Sen himself.

Geoffrey Hawthorn
Clare Hall Cambridge, 1986

NOTES

[1] I am grateful to Nick von Tunzelmann for drawing my attention to this paper and indeed for enabling me to catch up with the whole debate. Tunzelmann (1985) includes a review of the now considerable literature on it. I am also grateful to Roderick Floud for drawing my attention to his own work.

[2] This example comes from a lecture, 'Poverty: current theories and policies', given by Peter Townsend at the University of Warwick in March 1986 and the text of which he kindly let me see. The research on which it rests, in which Townsend himself is involved, is on poverty and the labour market in London in 1986.

[3] To call this question 'prior' may seem to commit one to 'atomism', to that belief in extensionless subjects and presuppositionless bearers of rights, inclined to anarchism, to which many non-economists suspect that economists are committed and to which some economists themselves can often seem to subscribe. It is therefore perhaps worth pointing out that even the most insistent critics of such atomism agree that one has to start with the self; they insist merely that 'the free individual cannot be concerned purely with his individual choices and the associations formed from such choices to the neglect of the matrix in which such choices can be open or closed, rich or meagre'; and that 'it is important to him that certain activities and institutions flourish in society' (Taylor 1985:207). Whatever may be true of the arguments of others, it is plain that Sen's, far from closing off such considerations, require them.

AMARTYA SEN

The Standard of Living: Lecture I, Concepts and Critiques*

It is hard to think of an idea more immediate than that of the living standard. It figures a good deal in everyday thought. It is, in fact, one of the few economic concepts that is not commonly greeted with the uncommon scepticism reserved for the other concepts of economics, such as 'perfect competition', or 'general equilibrium', or 'consumers' surplus', or 'social cost', or the almost supernatural 'M3'. While people are not prone to ask each other, 'How is your standard of living these days?' (at least, not yet), we do not believe we are indulging in technicalities when we talk about the living standard of the pensioners, or of the nurses, or of the miners, or – for that matter – of the chairman of the Coal Board. The standard of living communicates, and does so with apparent ease.

And yet the idea is full of contrasts, conflicts and even contradictions. Within the general notion of the living standard, divergent and rival views of the goodness of life co-exist in an unsorted bundle. There are many fundamentally different ways of seeing the quality of living, and quite a few of them have some immediate plausibility. You could be *well off*, without being *well*. You could be *well*, without being able to lead the life you *wanted*. You could have got the life you *wanted*, without being *happy*. You could be *happy*, without having much *freedom*. You could have a good deal of *freedom*, without *achieving* much. We can go on.

*In preparing these lectures I had the benefit of past discussions with Kenneth Arrow, Eva Colorni, Ronald Dworkin, John Hicks, John Muellbauer, John Rawls, T. M. Scanlon, Ian White and Bernard Williams. In revising them for publication, I have been much aided by the remarks of the discussants of these Tanner Lectures (Keith Hart, Ravi Kanbur, John Muellbauer and Bernard Williams), of Geoffrey Hawthorn, who directed that seminar, and by the later comments of Sudhir Anand and Martha Nussbaum.

1

Diversity is indeed part of the traditional picture of the living standard. Our job is not so much to evade it, but to face the diversity squarely and to find our way through it by drawing on the motivation underlying the interest in, and the use of, the concept of the standard of living. The living standard cannot be defined completely afresh by us 'professionals', and we must not sacrifice all the richness of the idea of the living standard to get something nicely neat and agreeably simple. There are too many associations and uses of the idea of the living standard for it to be treated as putty that can be refashioned as we like. We do, of course, have room for choice – indeed it is a *necessity* – given the contradictions among the different extant interpretations of the concept. But we must also relate our assessment and choice to pre-existing motivations and needs, while keeping the door open to meeting new demands and responding to untraditional problems.

COMPETITIVE AND CONSTITUTIVE PLURALITY

There are two rather different types of diversity in an idea like the standard of living, and it is useful to distinguish clearly between them. One type of diversity may be called 'competitive plurality'. Here different views stand as *alternatives* to each other. We can choose one of the rival views but not all of them (indeed not more than one). The other type is, in a sense, an *internal* diversity *within* a view, which may have different aspects that supplement but do not supplant each other. This may be called 'constitutive plurality'.

For example, if one view of the living standard sees it as *pleasure* and another as *opulence*, then this is an example of 'competitive plurality'. Of course, pleasure is not independent of opulence, but in their pure forms pleasure and opulence are *alternative* ways of seeing the living standard, even though there are associations, correlations and causal connections. In contrast, if one takes a general view of the living standard as, say, pleasure, then the non-commensurability of different *types* of pleasure – discussed by such authors as Plato, Aristotle and John Stuart Mill – suggests a 'constitutive plurality' within this general view.[1] Constitutive plurality involves seeing the living standard primarily as a basket of multiple attributes, even though secondarily that basket may quite possibly be given a

[1] This is discussed in Sen (1980–1). See also Gosling and Taylor (1982) and Nussbaum (1983–4).

numerical representation in the form of an index. Competitive plurality, on the other hand, is concerned with reflecting a choice over *alternative* baskets (each basket may have only one item *or* many). In facing diversities of outlook towards the standard of living, it is necessary to sort out the issues of competitive plurality from those of constitutive plurality.

In this first lecture I am concerned primarily with *competitive* plurality, and in particular with disputing the claims of certain traditional approaches to the standard of living. By the end of the lecture I would hope to have arrived at a moderate justification for an alternative approach. While these critical – and often negative – discussions will be concerned mainly with problems of 'choice' implicit in *competitive* plurality, issues of *constitutive* plurality will also be frequently involved, since some of the alternative approaches include pluralistic constructions of the concept of the living standard. In the second lecture I shall try to be more positive in exploring an alternative approach, which I have elsewhere called, in a related context, 'the capability approach' (Sen 1982; Sen 1984a: Essays 13, 14, 19, 20; Sen 1985a). The exploration and use of the capability approach will demand coming to grips with extensive constitutive plurality in seeing the living standard in the form of being able to achieve various personal conditions – to be able to do this or be that. It will also call for empirical illustrations to make sure that the approach can be sensibly and plausibly used in practical problems of living standard assessment.

OBJECTS AND STANDARDS

There are at least two basic questions in any evaluative exercise: (1) *What* are the objects of value? (2) *How* valuable are they? Strictly speaking, the first – what objects? – is an elementary aspect of the second – how valuable? The objects of value are those that will be positively valued when the valuational exercise is fully performed.[2]

---

[2] A few clarificatory points are called for here. First, an object may be one of value in a 'weak' sense, if it is potentially valuable, and actually valued in some cases but possibly not in all cases. When this weak formulation is used, the condition of 'dominance' (discussed later) would have to be correspondingly adapted. Second, an object that yields negative value can be made into an object of value through 'inversion', that is through treating it as an object of 'disvalue' and counting reduction rather than increase as an improvement. Third, if there is an object that is sometimes positively and sometimes negatively valued, there will arise a real

This may not, however, be the most helpful way of seeing the 'what' question. The more immediate sense of the question lies in the direct and intrinsic relevance of these objects in the assessment of the standard of living, and this relevance has to be distinguished from irrelevance on the one hand, and indirect or derivative relevance on the other.

To clarify the contrast, consider for the sake of illustration the general view of the standard of living as pleasure. This would indicate that pleasures of different types are the objects of value and that the standard of living consists of pleasures. Having a high income is not, then, an object of value in itself; nor is good health; nor the existence of a friendly bank manager who is ready to lend one money. These things may (indeed typically, will) influence one's standard of living, but that influence must work through some object of value – in this case, some type of pleasure. At the risk of oversimplification, it may be said that if an enhancement of some variable increases the standard of living, when everything else remains the same, then that variable is clearly an object of value in the evaluation of the standard of living.

Answering the 'what' question does take us some distance. We are able to say, for example, that if life style x has more of each of the objects of value than y has, then x involves a higher standard of living than y. The identification of objects of value yields a 'partial ordering', which can be characterised in different ways. Perhaps the simplest form is the following: if x has more of some object of value and no less of any than y, then x has a higher standard of living. I shall call this the 'dominance partial ordering'.

The dominance partial ordering is, of course, very familiar to economists in many contexts. In welfare economics it is employed to make *social* comparisons in terms of individual preferences or utilities, and it stands in that case for the so-called Pareto Principle: if someone has more utility in state x than in state y, and everyone has no less in x than in y, then x is socially better than y. That use of dominance reasoning is often thought to be uncontroversial, and

difficulty in pursuing the 'dominance' reasoning. In fact, the viability and usefulness of the distinction between identifying objects of value and the rest of the valuation exercise would be seriously compromised if such 'mixed' objects exist. This type of problem – and some others – are discussed in Sen (1975). But most 'mixed' cases tend to be *instrumentally* so (and not *intrinsically* valued positively in some cases and negatively in others). The problem may thus be avoidable, to a great extent, by going deeper. It is likely to be a more serious problem in the evaluation of 'opulence' than in evaluating 'functionings' and 'capabilities'.

indeed it would be so if the objects of value in deriving social rankings were exactly the set of individual utilities – no more and no less. Those of us who have disputed the uncontroversial nature of the Pareto Principle have done so on the basis of questioning its identification of value objects for social ranking (arguing that *non*-utility features may have intrinsic and direct relevance) (Sen 1970, 1977b, 1979a, 1979b). But the legitimacy of the 'dominance' reasoning itself has not been thus questioned. That particular controversy relates, of course, to the assessment of what is 'socially' appropriate, and not to the problem of the evaluation of the standard of living of a person or even of a group.

While the dominance partial ordering does take us some considerable distance, it is very unlikely that it would be adequate for making all the comparisons that we would want to make. When x has more of one object of value and y of another, then the dominance partial ordering will leave x and y unranked. To rank them the issue of the relative importance of the different objects has to be faced. What we then need are standards of comparison, giving us the relative forces exerted by the different objects of value in the valuation exercise. Dominance reasoning will need supplementation by reasoning that addresses the question of relative importance.

UTILITY, OBJECTS AND VALUATION METHODS

The utilitarian tradition provides a particular way of assessing the relative importance of different objects. Given the influence of this tradition in normative economics (through the works of such writers as Bentham, Mill, Jevons, Sidgwick, Edgeworth, Marshall and Pigou), it is not surprising that it is very often taken for granted that any evaluative concept in economics must be ultimately based on some notion or other of utility.[3] The standard of living is not taken to be an exception to this rule.

There are, however, two quite different ways of seeing the standard of living in terms of utility, and they do seem to get a bit confused in the welfare economic literature. One is based on seeing utility as an object of value itself. As A. C. Pigou put it, 'the elements of welfare are states of consciousness and, perhaps, their relations' (1952:10). In this

---

[3] For a powerful critique of this position, coming from one of the major figures in utility theory, see Hicks (1981). This consists of two extracts, respectively from *Essays in World Economics* (Oxford: Clarendon Press, 1959) and a paper read at Grenoble in 1961.

view, utility in the form of certain mental states is what is valuable, and indeed it is the only thing that is intrinsically valuable. The second view is to see utility as a valuational device which is used to evaluate *other* objects of value, for example goods possessed. As Pigou himself put it elsewhere, 'considering a single individual whose tastes are taken as fixed, we say that his dividend in period II is greater than in period I if the items that are added to it in period II are items he *wants more* than the items that are taken away from it in period II' (1952:51). Paul Samuelson puts the approach more succinctly: 'the real income of any person is said to be higher for batch of goods II than for I if II is higher up on his indifference or preference map' (1950:21).

It might be thought that if the indifference maps are based on utility totals then the two approaches must give the same rankings, and the valuation of goods by utility must coincide with the valuation of utility *per se*. But this is not so. Consider a person who ranks all commodity bundles in exactly the same way in periods I and II, in terms of utility, but gets more utility in period I from each bundle than in period II. In this case, it is quite possible for it to be the case that the utility value of bundle II is higher than that of bundle I in each period, and nevertheless the utility yield of bundle I actually enjoyed in period I is higher than the utility yield of bundle II actually enjoyed in period II. The respective utilities in descending order, then, may be the following, when $U_I(.)$ and $U_{II}(.)$ are the utility functions in the two periods, and x_I and x_{II} the respective commodity bundles:

$$U_I(x_{II})$$
$$U_I(x_I)$$
$$U_{II}(x_{II})$$
$$U_{II}(x_I)$$

If utility is used to evaluate commodities, then x_{II} must be ranked higher than x_I. Given the fulfilment of Pigou's condition of 'fixed tastes' (in the form of an unchanged 'indifference or preference map'), the living standard (in the form of real income) has to be seen as higher in the second period than in the first. If, on the other hand, living standard in the form of economic welfare is seen as utility itself ('states of consciousness', as Pigou puts it), then clearly it is higher in the first period than in the second, since $U_I(x_I) > U_{II}(x_{II})$. Valuation of commodity bundles *by* the index of utility is not the same exercise as the comparison of utility totals themselves. It does make a difference as to whether utility is the object of value itself, or only used to evaluate other objects of value.

In assessing the claims of utilities in the evaluation of the standard of living, both the possible uses (as objects of value and as valuational methods) have to be considered. And this makes the task particularly exacting since there are also at least three quite different ways of defining utility, namely pleasure, desire fulfilment and choice. So there are really at least six different boxes to examine.

UTILITY AS PLEASURE AND HAPPINESS

I start with the view of utility as pleasure. That term is used in many different senses. Some uses characterise pleasure rather narrowly, like John Selden's cheerless diagnosis: 'Pleasure is nothing but the intermission of pain'; or Dr Samuel Johnson's identification of the horns of an alleged dilemma: 'Marriage has many pains, but celibacy has no pleasures.' At the other end is the tendency in parts of the utilitarian tradition to assume that anything that is *valued*, must be, for that reason, a generator of pleasure, and the extent of pleasure will reflect well the strength of the valuation.

The utilitarian view does seem rather unlikely, since valuation is a reflective exercise with a complex and unstraightforward linkage with pleasure. Nevertheless, it is a suitably broad view of pleasures that we must seek in order to give any kind of plausibility to the pleasure view of well-being and the living standard. Jeremy Bentham's championing of the felicific calculus certainly did take a very broad view. It is only in a very broad sense that pleasure can possibly be seen as something like 'happiness' (and provide the basis of Bentham's 'the greatest happiness principle'). Marshall's and Pigou's use of the term 'satisfaction' is equally broad (Marshall 1949: Book 3; Pigou 1952: Chapter 2).

It is arguable that to think of satisfaction or happiness or pleasure as some kind of a homogeneous magnitude is simply a mistake, and that at best we have here a vector with different components related to different types of mental state and different causal influences.[4] But whether or not these different types of pleasure are seen as commensurable, there is no way of avoiding a broad-coverage view if the pleasure approach is to make a serious bid for being the basis of the living standard. The question is: even with a broad coverage, can this approach really make a *strong* bid?

It is quite easy to be persuaded that being happy is an achievement

---

[4] See particularly Scitovsky (1976).

that is valuable, and that in evaluating the standard of living, happiness is an object of value (or a collection of objects of value, if happiness is seen in a plural form). The interesting question regarding this approach is not the legitimacy of taking happiness to be valuable, which is convincing enough, but its *exclusive* legitimacy. Consider a very deprived person who is poor, exploited, overworked and ill, but who has been made satisfied with his lot by social conditioning (through, say, religion, or political propaganda, or cultural pressure). Can we possibly believe that he is doing well just because he is happy and satisfied? Can the living standard of a person be high if the life that he or she leads is full of deprivation? The standard of life cannot be so detached from the nature of the life the person leads. As an object of value, happiness or pleasure (even with a broad coverage) cannot possibly make a serious claim to *exclusive* relevance.

This takes us to the other way of using utility – not as an object of value, but as a method of valuation. However, this type of use is particularly unsuitable for the interpretation of utility as pleasure or happiness. Having pleasure or being happy is not a valuational activity as such, nor tightly tied to valuational activities. There is nothing perplexing in the remark: 'I still value x, but I haven't got it, and have learnt to be happy and satisfied without it.' While there are obvious connections between valuational activities and mental states of happiness, they cannot be identified with each other; nor can they be seen to be tied so firmly to each other that one can reasonably serve as a surrogate for the other.

It is, of course, possible to pack more into the notion of happiness than common usage will allow, and to see some objective achievements as part of being 'really happy'. If one were somehow stuck with having to make do with the notion of happiness, and base all evaluation on happiness alone, then this type of extension might well form a sensible exercise. Indeed, it is not surprising that such enrichment would appeal particularly to the self-declared utilitarian who has signed away his freedom to use other concepts. But that is a rather specialised interest.

The exercise also has a certain amount of general intellectual interest, particularly since the breadth and richness of the Greek concept of *eudaimonia* may suggest similarly broad interpretations of happiness or pleasure.[5] But in the present context there is not much

---

[5] See Gosling and Taylor (1982) and Nussbaum (1985).

point in going in that direction, since other notions of value and valuation can be entertained in their own right without their having to be inducted into serious consideration through riding on the back of pleasure or happiness. There are many other avenues that are explorable and deserve our direct attention. We have not signed away anything yet.

DESIRE AND CIRCUMSTANCES

What can we say about the interpretation of utility as desire fulfilment? While Pigou clearly did think that the importance of utility rests on satisfaction and not on desire, nevertheless he thought that strength of desire as reflected in demand will serve as good evidence for satisfaction. 'It is fair to suppose', he argued, 'that most commodities . . . will be desired with intensities proportioned to the satisfactions they are expected to yield' (1952:24).[6] This connection played an important part in Pigou's analysis of the living standard and economic welfare, making it possible for him to see them in terms of both satisfaction and desire, taking 'economic' welfare . . . to consist in that group of satisfactions and dissatisfactions which can be brought into relation with a money measure' (1952:23).

But if satisfaction is rejected as the basis of valuation, for reasons already outlined (or indeed for any other reason), then Pigou's defence of the *derived* importance of desires cannot be sustained. There is, however, a long tradition of attaching importance to the fulfilment of desire as such (not derivatively because it relates to satisfaction). It is also true that as an activity, desiring has a valuational aspect, which Frank Ramsey, among others, has emphasised (Ramsey 1926). Is it possible to claim that the desire interpretation provides an adequate valuational method (Hare 1981; Griffin 1982)? This claim has to be examined.

The relationship between valuing and desiring is a complex one.[7] Desiring may link closely with valuation, but it is not in itself a valuational activity. It is a plausible and frequent *consequence* of valuation, but desiring and valuing are not the same thing. There is nothing contradictory in asserting that one does not value something

---

[6] Pigou went on to discuss 'one very important exception' to 'this general conclusion', and this was concerned with *future* satisfactions given that 'our telescopic faculty is defective' (1952:25).

[7] I have discussed this and some related issues in Sen (1985b).

even though one desires it; or one does not value it as strongly as one's desire. Indeed, it would be baffling to identify the two, and say, for example: 'I must be valuing x highly since I desire x strongly.' If there is a link between desiring and valuing, it is certainly not one of identity.

Could it be that desiring is a *source* of value? This view may have some superficial attraction, but it is hard to see the relation between desiring and valuing in exactly that way. It is more perplexing to argue, 'I value x *because* I desire it', than to say the opposite, 'I desire x *because* I value it'. Valuing something is indeed an excellent ground for desiring it, and seen in this light, desiring is a natural consequence of valuing. It would be remarkable to turn this relationship on its head and see valuing as a consequence of desiring. 'Why do you value x?' she asks. I reply triumphantly, 'You see, it is because I *desire* it!' This would, of course, be a good way of earning a reputation for inscrutability, but not a particularly effective way of answering the question asked. There are, of course, some activities for which desiring is an important part of the activity itself (e.g., satisfying curiosity or making love), and in these cases desire must have an integral role in the process of valuation. But desire can scarcely be an adequate basis of valuation, in general.[8]

In fact, desiring plays a strategic role in making our wants credible and our aspirations viable. The importance of this aspect of the activity of desiring comes out sharply when *interpersonal* comparisons of desires are considered. It is not only that a poor person can offer less money for what he or she desires compared with a rich person, but also that even the strength of the mental force of desiring is influenced by the contingency of circumstances. The defeated and the down-trodden come to lack the courage to desire things that others more favourably treated by society desire with easy confidence. The absence of desire for things beyond one's means may not reflect any deficiency of valuing, but only an absence of hope, and a fear of

---

[8] The picture may look a little different in third-person contexts. The desire of *others* may be a good ground for us to value its fulfilment. This can be because *we value* that they get what *they value*, and their desire may tell us something about what they do value. (This *evidential* role is discussed later.) Or it can be that we value their happiness and know that desire fulfilment is conducive to happiness (and frustration a cause of suffering). One important difference between the first- and third-person cases lies in the fact that we have some responsibility for what *we* desire (and the need to relate it to what *we* value), whereas we have no such direct responsibility for the desire of others.

inevitable disappointment. The underdog comes to terms with social inequalities by bringing desires in line with feasibilities. The metric of desire does not, therefore, have much fairness; nor can it reflect the strength of valuations, especially what a person would value on serious and fearless reflection.

What is certainly easy to accept is that desire information has evidential value, in some contexts, in telling us about what a person does or does not value. This indeed is not without its use, and desires of *others* may even, for this evidential reason, provide a ground for support. But the jump from there to treating the strength of desire as the basis of valuation is a long and precarious one. The defects are particularly glaring in making *interpersonal* comparisons of well-being or of the standard of living. The point is not that interpersonal comparisons of desires cannot be scientifically made (as Lionel Robbins (1938) seems to have thought), but that they do not give us much help in making interpersonal comparisons of well-being or of living standard. The issue is *not* impossibility, but distortion.

As an object of value, desire fulfilment is, for reasons already discussed, very limited, if it is such an object at all. In assessing the well-being and the standard of living of a person, happiness may have direct relevance, and it is plausibly seen as one among various objects of value (as was discussed earlier). But the value of desire has to be assessed, and a person's desire for something he or she does not value correspondingly, and would not do so even on further reflection, may not be a good ground for counting it in the evaluation of that person's well-being or living standard (see Sen 1974, Broome 1978, Majumdar 1980, Pattainaik 1980, Winston 1980, Hollis 1981, van der Veen 1981, Goodin 1982, Hirschman 1982, McPherson 1982, Akerlof 1983, Elster 1983 and Schelling 1984).

It is also clear that the fulfilment of a person's desires may or may not be indicative of a high level of well-being or of living standard. The battered slave, the broken unemployed, the hopeless destitute, the tamed housewife, may have the courage to desire little, but the fulfilment of those disciplined desires is not a sign of great success and cannot be treated in the same way as the fulfilment of the confident and demanding desires of the better placed.

Desire fulfilment cannot, therefore, be the sole object of value (if it is an object of value at all), and as a valuational method it is very defective. The desire interpretation of utility may indeed be able to make stronger claims to providing a valuational method than the pleasure interpretation can (since desiring relates to valuing as an activity more immediately than having pleasure does), but these claims are not very strong either. Desiring is neither the same as valuing, nor is it a source of value in itself, nor a good indicator of what is (or should be) valued. Its valuational role is thus highly contingent and limited.[9]

CHOICE AND VALUATION

What about the third interpretation of utility – in terms of choice? The milder version of this approach, involving only 'ordinal' comparisons, claims that if you choose x when y is available, then x has higher utility for you than y. Stronger versions derive 'cardinal' measures of utility from choice involving more demanding behaviour patterns (e.g., over lotteries). Choice behaviour is, of course, of much interest on its own. But as an interpretation of well-being, the binary relation underlying choice is very strained.[10] It confounds choosing with benefiting, and it does this by what looks like a definitional trick. The popularity of this view in economics may be due to a mixture of an obsessive concern with observability and a peculiar belief that choice (in particular, market choice) is the only human aspect that can be observed.

Choice is obviously a very different type of activity from valuation, and in so far as it has a connection with valuation, this must partly arise from choice being a *reflection* of desire. Thus, much of what was said about the desire interpretation of utility will apply here too,[11] except, perhaps, the point about the bias of the desire interpretation against the unfavoured underdog in making *interpersonal* comparisons based on desire *intensities*. In fact, the choice interpretation does not immediately yield any practical method of interpersonal comparison whatever. Each person makes his or her own choices, and interpersonal comparisons of utility cannot come out of the observation of actual choices of different individuals. It is possible to extend this approach to imaginary choices, for example 'Would you

---

[9] These questions have been further discussed in Sen (1985b).
[10] This issue is discussed in Sen (1977a). There may not, of course, be such a binary relation if the choice function proves to be 'non-binary'. But the deeper problem concerns the *interpretation* of the binary relation *even when* the choice function may be binary.
[11] See Broome (1978).

rather be person i or person j given the choice?', and such a format has been elegantly used by Vickrey, Harsanyi and others to derive some kind of interpersonal comparisons (Vickrey 1945, Harsanyi 1955).[12] But the relevance of such counterfactual choices is not clear, and the answers are difficult to interpret and build on. The choice interpretation is generally quite a strained one anyway, and it gets completely out of breath when trying to scale the heights of interpersonal comparisons.

There is a further difficulty with the choice interpretation. What you choose must depend on your motivation. While the pursuit of one's own well-being is a good enough motivation, it is not of course the only possible one. If you do something for national pride, the glory of your football team, or the benefit of your great aunt, its impact on your well-being may be quite secondary and derivative, with the main force behind your choice relating to something else. Under these circumstances, to treat choice as a reflector of your well-being is surely to overlook the motivational complexity of choice behaviour.

To some extent the same problem arises with the desire interpretation also, since you may desire to do something not because it is particularly good for you, but for some other reason. It is, of course, quite plausible to believe that a failure to achieve what one would choose, or to get what one desires, is likely to affect the value of one's well-being adversely. Disappointment, frustration, and suffering from a sense of failure may well reduce a person's well-being, no matter what he aims to achieve. But it is hard to be persuaded that the impact on the person's well-being is well reflected by the intensity of desire or the metric of choice, since the basic motivation is not avoidance of disappointment or frustration, but something else like national glory or some social or political ideal.

We must conclude that none of the interpretations of utility (pleasure, desire fulfilment, choice) takes us very far in pinning down well-being or the living standard, and the failure applies both to seeing them as objects of value and to taking them to be valuational methods. They do, of course, have connections with well-being and

---

[12] See also Suppes (1966) and Arrow (1963:114–15). Though the Suppes–Arrow analyses can be interpreted in a 'choice' framework for utility, there is no necessity to do so, and the formal analysis is, in fact, consistent with each interpretation of utility. Furthermore, much of it is extendible also to non-utility interpretations of well-being (including those of 'the capability approach', to be investigated here).

living standard, enough to give some superficial plausibility to the utility-based ways of seeing the standard of living. Happiness clearly is an *object of value* in the living standard (though by no means the only one), and desire and choice do have some evidential importance in giving information on valuation (though with ambiguities and systematic biases). Utility and living standard *are* related, but they are second cousins rather than siblings.

OPULENCE, COMMODITIES, FUNCTIONINGS AND CAPABILITIES

The failure of utility to get very far, and the role of 'subjectivism' in this failure, may well push us in the direction of more objective considerations. In that context, the advantages of seeing living standard in terms of commodity possession and opulence might appear to be serious enough. Indeed, that is the way 'real income' is typically viewed, and the link between real income and living standard must be fairly close. As it happens, even Pigou argued that in determining 'a national minimum standard of real income' below which people should not have to fall, 'it must be conceived, not as a subjective minimum of satisfaction, but as an objective minimum of conditions'. He then proceeded to characterise this minimum in terms of commodity possessions: 'The minimum includes some defined quantity and quality of house accommodation, of medical care, of education, of food, of leisure, of the apparatus of sanitary convenience and safety where work is carried on, and so on.'[13]

Pigou did, in fact, go on to discuss the plausibility of the promotion of utility, in the form of 'economic welfare', by the establishment of some 'minimum standard', and to enquire 'by *what* minimum standard it will be promoted most effectively'. Thus the 'objective' approach of minimum real income was meant to have been ultimately based on the pursuit of utility. But Pigou did not go very far along that line. He abandoned the linking exercise on the respectable and comforting (if somewhat puzzling) ground that to pursue that exercise 'it would be necessary to obtain and to analyse a mass of detailed information, much of which is not, in present circumstances, accessible to students' (1952:76).

If we are to move in the objectivist direction, is this the right way to go? There cannot be much doubt that the list of minimum require-

[13] Pigou (1952:759). Cooter and Rappoport (1984) have recently discussed the 'material welfare' basis of the work of many traditional utilitarian economists.

ments presented by Pigou has a good deal of immediate plausibility and, more generally, it does seem sensible to be concerned with the possession of vitally important commodities in understanding the living standard. Indeed, it is easy to argue that it is more plausible to identify someone as having a low standard of living on the ground that he or she is deprived of decent housing, or adequate food, or basic medical care, than on the ground that he or she is simply unhappy or frustrated. As a direction to go, concentration on the possession of vital commodities seems fair enough.[14]

The more exacting question is not whether this is the right direction to go, but whether taking stock of commodity possession is the right place to stop. Opulence in the form of commodity possession is undoubtedly important in enhancing the standard of living, but is the standard of living best seen as opulence *itself*? Earlier on in this lecture a distinction was made between being 'well off' and being 'well', and it is reasonable to argue that while well-being is related to being well off, they are not the same and may possibly diverge a good deal.[15]

The distinction needs to be further probed. Consider two persons *A* and *B*. Both are quite poor, but *B* is poorer. *A* has a higher income and succeeds in particular in buying more food and consuming more of it. But *A* also has a higher metabolic rate and some parasitic disease, so that despite his higher food consumption, he is in fact more undernourished and debilitated than *B* is. Now the question: Who has the higher standard of living of the two? It is not, I believe, a $64,000 question (or, if it is, then money is easy to earn). *A* may be richer or

---

[14] When discussing socially widespread deprivation (e.g. famines), focusing on entitlement failures (in particular, failures in the ability to command food on the part of large sections of the population) may provide an adequate starting point of analysis, and may provide a simple contrast with more aggregative and supply-centred analyses of such phenomena (e.g. in terms of a decline of total food availability). The advantages of the entitlement focus have been discussed elsewhere (see, for example, Sen 1981 and Tilly 1983). But as a view of the living standard as such, concentration on entitlements is rather crude and rough, the merits of that approach being relevant in a different context, for example in providing an understanding of the causation of famines.

[15] One interesting case of divergence may relate to the well-known controversy on the impact of early industrialisation on the standard of living of the British working class. It appears that in the period 1780–1820, the death rate fell quite steadily, while measures of the opulence of the British working class showed little rise, whereas during 1820–40, as opulence did seem to increase a little, the fall of the death rate was halted and reversed. For a lucid account of this controversy (including the contrary movements), see Deane (1969: Chapter 15). On the main lines of the controversy, see also Hobsbawm (1957), Hartwell (1961), and Hartwell and Hobsbawm (1963).

more opulent, but it cannot really be said that he has the higher standard of living of the two, since he is quite clearly more undernourished and more debilitated. The standard of living is not a standard of opulence, even though it is *inter alia* influenced by opulence. It must be directly a matter of the life one leads rather than of the resources and means one has to lead a life. The movement in the objectivist direction away from utility may be right, but opulence is not the right place to settle down.

The variation of nourishment *vis-à-vis* food intake is influenced by a variety of physiological, medical, climatic and social factors. To reach the same level of nutrition as another, one needs a larger command over food if one has a higher metabolic rate (or a larger body frame), or if one is pregnant (or breast-feeding), or if one has a disease that makes absorption more difficult, or if one lives in a colder climate, or if one has to toil a lot, or if food has other uses (such as for entertainment, ceremonies or festivals). Pigou's move in the direction of food possession was clearly right, but the concern is not so much with food as such but with the type of life one succeeds in living with the help of food and other commodities, for example whether one can be well nourished, whether one has the ability to entertain, and so on.

The same applies to other types of commodity and other functionings – or living conditions – that are helped by these commodities. While Marx's (1887) attack on 'commodity fetishism' was made in a rather different context, that attack is deeply relevant to the concept of the standard of living as well. The market values commodities, and our success in the material world is often judged by our opulence; but despite that, commodities are no more than means to other ends. Ultimately, the focus has to be on what life we lead and what we can or cannot do, can or cannot be. I have elsewhere called the various living conditions we can or cannot achieve, our 'functionings', and our ability to achieve them, our 'capabilities' (Sen 1984a: Introduction and Chapters 13–20). The main point here is that the standard of living is really a matter of functionings and capabilities, and not a matter directly of opulence, commodities or utilities.

This approach goes back not only to Marx, but also to Adam Smith. In fact, despite the frequent claim that Adam Smith was mainly concerned with 'wealth maximisation', there is much evidence that he was deeply concerned with avoiding concentration on commodities (and wealth) as such, and keen on escaping the fetishism of which Marx spoke later.[16] In fact, Adam Smith went well beyond the standard characterisations of living conditions and considered such functionings as not being 'ashamed to appear in public', and analysed how the commodity requirements for this achievement – clothing, shoes, etc. – varied with social customs and cultural norms (Smith 1910:351–3). These customs and norms are, in their turn, influenced by the economic conditions of the respective societies. In analysing these relationships, Adam Smith not only distanced his own approach from commodity fetishism and wealth maximisation, but also showed the social nature of these relationships between commodities (and opulence), on the one hand, and capabilities (and achievements of living conditions), on the other. The same capability of being able to appear in public without shame has variable demands on commodities and wealth, depending on the nature of the society in which one lives.

THE RELATIVE AND THE ABSOLUTE

I shall explore further the capability approach to the standard of living in the second lecture. I end this mainly negative discussion by a few remarks on international variations in what is taken to be poverty, and the use of minimum living standards for the identification of the poor. There has been a lively debate on the relative nature of the standards of poverty and the need to revise upwards the cut-off line as we go up the ladder of general opulence. Some have tried to give this variation a fairly simple and direct form. For example, Peter Townsend has argued: 'Lacking an alternative criterion, the best assumption would be to relate sufficiency to the average rise (or fall) in real incomes' (Townsend 1979a, 1979b; see also Fiegehen, Lansley and Smith 1977, Beckerman and Clark 1982, Townsend 1985 and Sen 1985c). Others have seen in such relativity a confounding of poverty and inequality, arguing that poverty would then appear to be pretty much impossible to eliminate. If the poverty line is fixed entirely relatively to the 'average' income, there are always some who are relatively poor.[17] Still others have gone on to seek

---

[16] On two different views on the approach of 'wealth maximisation', see Posner (1972) and Dworkin (1980).

[17] This is not, strictly speaking, correct. Even if the poverty line is defined entirely relatively to the mean income or the median income (say, 60% of it), it is still possible for poverty to be eliminated, though that would depend on the elimination of a type of inequality. If, on the other hand, the 'poor' are defined as those in, say, the bottom decile of the population, then poverty will obviously not be eliminable.

peculiar psychological explanations for the popularity of the relativist view. For example, Dr Rhodes Boyson, as Minister of Social Security, had the following to say in Parliament recently: 'Those on the poverty line in the United States earn more than 50 times the average income of someone in India. That is what relative poverty is all about . . . Apparently, the more people earn, the more they believe poverty exists, presumably so that they can be pleased about the fact that it is not themselves who are poor.'[18]

The mystification involved in this extraordinary speculation can be substantially eliminated if we see the standard of living in terms of functionings and capabilities. Some capabilities, such as being well nourished, may have more or less similar demands on commodities (such as food and health services) irrespective of the average opulence of the community in which the person lives. Other capabilities, such as the ones with which Adam Smith was particularly concerned, have commodity demands that vary a good deal with average opulence. To lead a life without shame, to be able to visit and entertain one's friends, to keep track of what is going on and what others are talking about, and so on, requires a more expensive bundle of goods and services in a society that is generally richer, and in which most people have, say, means of transport, affluent clothing, radios or television sets, etc. Thus, some of the same capabilities (relevant for a 'minimum' level of living) require more real income and opulence in the form of commodity possession in a richer society than in poorer ones. The same absolute levels of capabilities may thus have a greater relative need for incomes (and commodities). There is thus no mystery in the necessity of having a 'relativist' view on the space of incomes even when poverty is defined in terms of the same *absolute* levels of basic capabilities. Rhodes Boyson's far-fetched psychological explanation is completely redundant.

There are, of course, other variations as well in the comparative picture. Sometimes the same goods may cost relatively more, in terms of exchange rates of currencies, in the richer countries than in the poorer ones, as has been well discussed by Dan Usher (1968). Also, the level of *capabilities* that are accepted as 'minimum' may themselves be upwardly revised as the society becomes richer and more and more people achieve levels of capabilities not previously reached by many (Sen 1981: Chapters 2, 3; see also Hobsbawm 1968 and Wedderburn

---

[18] *Hansard*, 28 June 1984. These and other views on poverty are critically discussed by Mack and Lansley (1985).

1974). These variations add further to the need for more income in the richer countries to avoid what is seen as poverty in terms of 'contemporary standards'.

There is no great difficulty in sorting out the different elements in the relativity of the poverty line in the space of incomes (and that of commodities) once the conception of the standard of living is given an adequate formulation in terms of capabilities. A difficult, but central, issue in studying poverty is the concept of the standard of living itself.[19]

PLURALITY AND ASSESSMENT

I began this lecture by making a distinction between 'competitive plurality' and 'constitutive plurality'. Much of this lecture has been concerned with sorting out some substantive issues of *competitive* plurality in the idea of the standard of living. In trying to develop a particular way of seeing the standard of living, critical – and frequently negative – positions have been taken regarding the relevance and adequacy of competing claimants – opulence, happiness, desire fulfilment, choice. However, while arguing for the rejection of these other views of the living standard, I have also tried to clarify and explore both their correlative associations and their causal connections with the living standard.

The role of functionings and capabilities in the concept of the living standard will be further analysed and examined in the second lecture. Since there are many types of functionings and capabilities, the question of *constitutive* plurality is particularly important and challenging in this context.[20] Though the capability approach does not lead to one particular theory of valuation (but defines instead a class of such theories within a general motivational structure), nevertheless the principles underlying the valuation will require close investigation and scrutiny. That is one of the tasks for the second lecture.

---

[19] This is discussed in Sen (1983a).

[20] This constitutive plurality, related to *personal* living standard, will need supplementation by problems of constitutive plurality involved in social aggregation, when the focus is on *social* living standard. The latter question is discussed in Sen (1976a, 1976b). While these aggregation problems are defined there in the spaces of incomes and commodity holdings, they can be correspondingly reformulated in the spaces of functionings and capabilities as well.

AMARTYA SEN

The Standard of Living: Lecture II, Lives and Capabilities

There are two major challenges in developing an appropriate approach to the evaluation of the standard of living. First, it must meet the motivation that makes us interested in the concept of the living standard, doing justice to the richness of the idea. It is an idea with far-reaching relevance, and we cannot just redefine it in some convenient but arbitrary way. Second, the approach must nevertheless be practical in the sense of being usable for actual assessments of the living standard. This imposes restrictions on the kinds of information that can be required and the techniques of evaluation that may be used.

These two considerations – relevance and usability – pull us, to some extent, in different directions. Relevance may demand that we take on board the inherent complexities of the idea of the living standard as fully as possible, whereas usability may suggest that we try to shun complexities if we reasonably can. Relevance wants us to be ambitious; usability urges restraint. This is, of course, a rather common conflict in economics, and while we have to face the conflict squarely, we must not make heavy weather of it.

MEASUREMENT AND MOTIVATION

In fact, that conflict was well understood by the pioneers of the subject. It is fair to say that the discipline of statistical measurement of the living standard began with Sir William Petty and his book *Political Arithmetick*, written around 1676, but published posthumously in 1691. Petty's interests were wide. He was Professor of Anatomy at Oxford and Professor of Music at Gresham College. He invented the 'double-bottomed' ship, which alas was lost in a storm.

He restored to life a woman who had been hanged for infanticide, which gave Petty some undeserved notoriety. He presented his *Political Arithmetick* to Charles II, but it was judged to be too offensive to France to be published then.

The motivation for Petty's national income estimation was clearly a better understanding of the condition of life of the people. His statistical analysis was meant 'to show' that 'the King's subjects are not in so bad a condition as discontented Men would make them'. His view of the condition of people was broad enough to include 'the Common Safety' and 'each Man's particular Happiness'.[1] But he was also realistic enough about measurement problems to concentrate almost exclusively on opulence when it came to estimation. The national income, as an index of opulence, was estimated with the use of both the 'income method' and the 'expenditure method', in somewhat rudimentary forms.

In fact, Petty was dead keen on the importance of accurate measurements. He was a great quantifier and very doubtful about what he called 'intellectual Arguments'. He declared proudly that 'instead of using only comparative and superlative words, and intellectual Arguments', he would choose to express himself 'in Terms of Number, Weight, or Measure'. As one of the first members of the Royal Society, he had argued strongly against vague generalisations, and in an eloquent statement that would, I suppose, warm the hearts of some of the purer quantitative economists of today, Petty suggested that in discussions in the Royal Society 'no word might be used but what marks either number, weight, or measure'.[2] Perhaps the miserable practitioner of 'intellectual Arguments' might be tempted to claim that Petty's suggestion had a modest weight, a minute measure and a wee number.

But Petty was, of course, quite right to keep the measurement issue firmly in view in his studies of the national income and living standard. He combined a clear account of the motivation for the measurement (related to living conditions and happiness) with opting for the tangible and the tractable in his totting-up. That focus on quantification was retained by the stalwarts that followed him, including Gregory King, François Quesnay, Antoine Lavoisier, Joseph Louis Lagrange, and others. Lavoisier was, in his own way, as

---

[1] These and other quotations below come from C. H. Hull's edition of Petty's writings (Hull 1899:313).
[2] See Hull (1899:lxiv).

uncompromising as Petty in insisting on quantification. The lack of quantification, he thought, was what ailed political economy: 'This science like many others began with metaphysical discussions: its theory has advanced; but its practice is still in its infancy, and the statesman lacks at all times the facts on which to base his speculations'.[3] He also had great confidence that national income analysis and quantitative studies of the living standard would settle all disputes in political economy and indeed make that subject redundant: 'A work of this nature will contain in a few pages the whole science of political economy; or, rather, it would do away with the further need for this science; because the results will become so clear, so palpable, the different questions that could be raised would be so easily solved, that there would no longer be any difference of opinion'.[4]

Lagrange, sticking in his turn to dedicated quantification, introduced an innovation the import of which can be fully understood only with very recent developments in the analysis of consumption in terms of 'characteristics', due to Gorman (1956) and Lancaster (1966). Lagrange converted goods that had similar roles in consumption into equivalents of each other in terms of their characteristics. In particular, he converted vegetal foods into units of wheat in terms of nourishment value, all meat into equivalents of beef, and as a good Frenchman, all beverages into units of wine.

No less importantly, Lagrange took note of the different needs for different nutrients by different groups of consumer, needs which he related to occupation, location and the like, and specified for different groups different ratios of vegetable and meat requirements.[5] What is particularly interesting in the context of the issues discussed in my last lecture, Lagrange was not only reducing commodities into characteristics, but also assessing – albeit rather crudely – the value of the commodities in terms of what it did to the lives of the people consuming them. Whereas Adam Smith was the pioneer in showing the varying relation between opulence and achievements of *social* functionings (as was discussed in the first lecture), the mathematician Lagrange, who was Smith's contemporary, played a similarly pio-

---

[3] *Oeuvres de Lavoisier* (Paris, 1893), Vol. 6, 404–5; English translation from Studenski (1958: Part I, 70).

[4] *Oeuvres* (1893), Vol. 6, 415–16; English translation from Studenski (1958: Part I, 71).

[5] See E. Daire and de Molinari, *Mélanges d'économie politique* (Paris, 1847) and C. Ganilh, *La Théorie de l'économie politique* (Paris, 1815), discussed by Studenski (1958: Part I, 75–6).

neering role in pursuing the variability of *physical* functionings *vis-à-vis* food intakes, depending on activities, locations, and the like. If the perspective of functionings and capabilities has been neglected in the literature on real income and living standard, the reason for this cannot be found in the absence of early initiatives in that direction.[6]

In general, Lagrange also thought that food statistics gave a better idea of a country's well-being and poverty than a more comprehensive measure of national income, and he concentrated his efforts on getting the food picture as accurate and exhaustive as possible, including such items as fruits and garden vegetables, which had been neglected by Lavoisier and others. The motivational basis of real income estimation was thus strengthened and refined by Lagrange in a direction that is particularly important for studies of the living conditions of the poor.

The statistical format of national income has been developed a good deal since the days of Petty, King, Lavoisier and Lagrange, and a great many complexities have been handled with ingenuity and skill.[7] National income accounting does, of course, have to play quite a variety of roles in economic analysis, going well beyond its relevance to living standard and involving such matters as macro-economic investigations of output and activity, studies of saving, investment and growth, examination of productivity and efficiency, and so on. It is, therefore, not surprising that the links with the assessment of the standard of living are often relatively remote.

In fact, it is obvious enough that in order to pursue the notion of the living standard as such, we have to rely also on other types of statistics in addition to whatever we get from national accounting.[8] There are two distinct reasons for this. First, as was argued in the first lecture, the living standard is not just a matter of opulence, even though there

[6] In a general sense, the perspective of 'functionings' in assessing social arrangements can, in fact, be traced much further back, at least to Aristotle (see his *Politics*, and *Nicomachean Ethics*). I am grateful to Martha Nussbaum for drawing my attention to the existence and importance of this Aristotelian connection.

[7] For a taste of various types of problem faced and solutions proposed, see Meade and Stone (1957), Samuelson and Swamy (1974) and Hicks (1981). See also Kuznets (1966), Hicks (1971) and Kravis, Heston and Summers (1978).

[8] Examples of illuminating use of data regarding physical stature for historical analysis of the living standard can be found in a number of recent contributions, for example Floud and Wachter (1982), and Fogel, Engerman and Trussell (1982). The use of data on physical stature for the assessment of contemporary undernourishment and the living standard can also be found in several empirical studies. Examples of its application in India include, *inter alia*, Gopalan (1984), Sen and Sengupta (1983), and UNICEF (1984).

are causal connections. Second, the particular way of characterising opulence that would be most suitable for living standard analysis through causal and other associations may not be the most useful for the other purposes which national accounting also has to cater for. There is a need for more specialised accounting when investigating the living standard.

NEEDS, INDICATORS AND FOUNDATIONAL QUESTIONS

Such specialised accounting has, in fact, been much encouraged in recent years by the emergence of the so-called 'basic needs' approach and by the work done by writers on 'social indicators'.[9] These developments have tended to emphasise the importance of those features of the economy that relate closely to the fulfilment of what have been seen as the 'basic needs' of the people, paying attention also to aspects of social achievements that go well beyond the growth of GNP only. These developments can, to some extent, be seen as something of a return to the original motivation that led the pioneers to develop national income measures, for, as we have seen, they too were much influenced by the need to investigate the basis of good living conditions.

From the perspective of functionings and capabilities, these developments are moves in the right direction. It is, of course, true that 'basic needs' are typically formulated in terms of *commodity possession* (rather than functioning achievements) and that social indicators include a great many indices that have little to do with the functionings and capabilities of the people in question. But the net impact of the emergence of these approaches has been to draw attention, in an immediate and powerful way, to the importance of the type of life that people are able to lead.

An emphasis on basic needs can, of course, be justified in many different ways, and the 'basic needs' approach does not go much into this foundational aspect of the problem. The items in Pigou's list of a 'national minimum standard of real income' (Pigou 1952: Part IV, 758–67), discussed in the last lecture (including minimum accommodation, food, medical care, education, etc.), are clearly specifications

---

[9] The literature is by now quite vast. For some of the arguments and examples of basic needs and social indicators, see Adelman and Morris (1973), Sen (1973), Streeten and Burki (1978), Grant (1978), Morris (1979), Chichilnisky (1980), Streeten *et al.* (1981) and Wells (1983).

of basic needs, done much before the alleged birth of the basic needs approach. Any practical analysis of the living standard must pay some attention to these features, no matter what the ultimate justification for the attention is. In Pigou's case, the ultimate justification was utility, even though – as was discussed in the first lecture – Pigou stopped short of providing the connecting analysis.

The strategic relevance of basic needs is not a controversial matter. What is open to debate and disputation is the *foundation* of this concern. Are basic needs important *because and only because* their fulfilment contributes to utility? If not, *why* are they important? Closely related to this question of justification is the issue of the *form* in which basic needs have to be seen. Are they best seen in terms of *commodities* that people may be reasonably expected to possess (typically the chosen form in the basic needs literature)? This would relate nicely to some extended sense of opulence and to a justification in terms of the value of popular opulence. But is that justification easy to accept? Why should we be concerned – not just strategically but fundamentally – with opulence, rather than with what people succeed in doing or being? And if it is accepted that the concern is basically with the kind of lives people do lead or can lead, then this must suggest that the 'basic needs' should be formulated in line with functionings and capabilities. If they are, for some reason, stated in the form of commodity requirements, the derivative and contingent nature of that formulation must be given adequate recognition. If the objects of value are functionings and capabilities, then the so-called 'basic' needs in the form of commodity requirements are *instrumentally* (rather than intrinsically) important. The main issue is the goodness of the life that one can lead. The need of commodities for any specified achievement of living conditions may vary greatly with various physiological, social, cultural and other contingent features, as was discussed in the first lecture.[10] The value of the living standard lies in the living, and not in the possessing of commodities, which has derivative and varying relevance.

The purpose of making these distinctions is not to chastise the 'basic needs approach', which has in fact played a positive part in challenging the overemphasis on GNP and economic growth. But it is a mistake to see it as a deeply founded approach. It needs support, and this support can come from various quarters, including from utility

[10] For an interesting study of the relevance of variations of needs in perceptions of distributive justice, see Yaari and Bar-Hillel (1984:8–12).

(as argued by Pigou), or from the value of functionings and capabilities (as argued here). The typical formulation of basic needs in terms of commodity requirements is a specification in terms of required opulence, and like opulence in general, these so-called 'basic needs' belong to an *intermediate* stage of the analysis. So long as we understand this role (and recognise the necessity of the parametric variability of commodity-based 'basic needs'), we can appreciate the usefulness of the basic needs approach without losing sight of deeper questions.

LIVING STANDARD AND WELL-BEING

I have so far not discussed explicitly the distinction between the concept of well-being and that of the standard of living, and that issue should now be faced before proceeding further. Well-being is the broader and more inclusive of the two related notions. Pigou tried to draw a distinction between 'economic welfare' and 'total welfare', defining the former as 'that part of social welfare that can be brought directly or indirectly into relation with the measuring-rod of money' (1952:11). His distinction is ambiguous and rather unhelpful, and it may not serve the purpose for which Pigou devised it. In fact, some of the obviously 'non-economic' aspects of well-being may also, in some sense, 'be brought directly or indirectly into relation with the measuring-rod of money', for example through such 'vulgar' questions as: how much would you be willing to pay to be loved by your granddaughter? These payments may not actually be made, but nor are some obviously 'economic' ones (e.g., how much would you pay to eliminate urban air pollution that adds to the cost of keeping your house clean?). The interpretation of the information content of answers to these questions is deeply problematic. Similarly, other payments that happen to be actually made may not be geared to one's own well-being at all, and thus not figure in one's 'economic well-being', for example donations made to OXFAM for famine relief possibly without any direct or indirect benefit to oneself. While it is easy to be sympathetic to the reasons that prompted Pigou to make the distinction between 'economic welfare' and 'total welfare', the nature of that distinction is confusing and its usability quite limited.

One way of amending Pigou's distinction in line with his evident motivation is to separate out 'material' functionings and capabilities (e.g., to be well-nourished) from others (e.g., being wise and contented). I have tried to argue elsewhere (Sen 1984b) that this may well be a good way to proceed, but I am less sure of this now. Being psychologically well-adjusted may not be a 'material' functioning, but it is hard to claim that that achievement is of no intrinsic importance to one's standard of living. In fact, any achievement that is rooted in the life that one oneself leads (or can lead), rather than arising from other objectives, does have a claim to being directly relevant to one's standard of living. It is possible that this way of drawing the line is a little too permissive, but the alternatives that have been proposed seem clearly too narrow. For example, the 'economic test' of whether a deprivation can be eradicated by more affluence is tempting enough, but it is hard to claim that the standard of living of a person dying of an incurable disease (not remediable by affluence) is not directly reduced by that particular predicament. The living standard may, often enough, be influenceable by economic means, but that is more plausibly seen not as the basis of a sound *definition* of the standard of living, but as an important *empirical* statement about the typical relationship between economic means and the living standard.

If the line of distinction proposed here is accepted, then the contrast between a person's well-being and living standard must arise from possible influences on personal well-being coming from sources other than the nature of one's life. For example, one's misery at the sorrow of another certainly does reduce *ceteris paribus* one's well-being, but in itself this is not a reduction in the person's living standard. This contrast has featured in practical discussions for a very long time. For example, in the third century BC, Emperor Aśoka notes the distinction clearly enough in one of his 'rock edicts' in the context of clarifying the idea of an injury being done to a person: 'And, if misfortune befalls the friends, acquaintances, companions and relations of persons who are full of affection [towards the former], even though they are themselves well provided for, [this misfortune] is also an injury to their own selves' (Rock Edict XIII at Erragudi, Statement VII; see Sircar 1979:34). One's well-being may be affected through various influences, and it is the assessment of the nature of the life the person himself leads that forms the exercise of evaluation of the living standard.

It may be useful to see the distinction in the context of another contrast, to wit that between a person's overall achievements (whatever he wishes to achieve as an 'agent'), and his personal well-being (elaborated in my Dewey lectures (Sen 1985b)). Three different notions may be distinguished: (1) agency achievement, (2) personal well-being, and (3) the standard of living.[11] The distinction between agency achievement and personal well-being arises from the fact that a person may have objectives other than personal well-being. If, for example, a person fights successfully for a cause, making great personal sacrifice (even perhaps giving his or her life for it), then this may be a big agency achievement without being a corresponding achievement of personal well-being. In the second distinction, namely that between well-being and the living standard, we are restricted in both cases to looking at achievements of personal well-being only, but whereas for well-being *tout court* there is no further qualification as to whether the achievement relates to the nature of the person's life, the notion of the standard of living does include exactly that qualification.

In an earlier paper (Sen 1977a) a distinction was made between 'sympathy' and 'commitment' in the context of analysing motivations for action. In helping another person, the reduction of the other's misery may have the net effect of making one feel – and indeed *be* – better off. This is a case of an action that can be promoted on grounds of 'sympathy' (whether or not that is why the action is actually chosen), and this falls *within* the general area of promotion of one's own well-being.[12] In contrast, a case of 'commitment' is observed when a person decides to do a thing (e.g., being helpful to another) despite its not being, in the net, beneficial to the agent himself. This would put the action outside the range of promoting one's own well-being (linking the action with *other* objectives). At the risk of oversimplification, it may be said that we move from agency achievement to personal well-being by narrowing the focus of attention through ignoring 'commitments', and we move from personal well-being to the standard of living by further narrowing the focus through ignoring 'sympathies' (and, of course, 'antipathies',

[11] I am grateful to Bernard Williams for suggesting this way of clarifying the distinction between well-being and living standard (though he would have, I understand, drawn the boundaries somewhat differently). Williams' suggestion came in the seminar following my Tanner Lectures, but I have taken the liberty of following up the idea in the lectures themselves, since it makes my line of reasoning easier to understand and assess. On related matters, see my 'Reply' (pp. 109–10).

[12] It is, however, important to distinguish between one's well-being being promoted by one's action and that action being chosen for that reason; on this, see Nagel (1970). Here we are concerned primarily with effects rather than with motivations, and thus the use of the distinction between 'sympathy' and 'commitment' is rather different here from its use in Sen (1977a).

and other influences on one's well-being from outside one's own life). Thus narrowed, personal well-being related to one's own life will reflect one's standard of living.

The lines of distinction can, of course, be drawn in other ways as well, but the system outlined here seems to be both interesting in itself *and* well related to the motivations underlying traditional concerns with the concept of the standard of living. The curiosity and interest – that made Petty, Lavoisier, Lagrange and others take up their investigations into real income and living standards were related to the assessment of the nature of people's lives. The view of the living standard taken here fits in fairly well with that motivation.

VALUATION AND FUNCTIONINGS

In assessing the standard of living of a person, the objects of value can sensibly be taken to be aspects of the life that he or she succeeds in living. The various 'doings' and 'beings' a person achieves are thus potentially all relevant to the evaluation of that person's living standard. But this is, of course, an enormous – possibly infinite – list, since a person's activities and states can be seen in so many different ways (and can also be persistently subdivided). Thus, the identification of certain 'doings' and 'beings' as objects of value is itself a valuational exercise – an issue that was touched on in the first lecture. The list of functionings reflects a view of what is valuable and what is of no intrinsic value (though possibly quite useful in the pursuit of other things of value).

The assessment of living standard would, of course, have to go beyond this initial identification. It might even appear that no comparisons at all of *overall* living conditions can be made without going beyond that identification into more specific valuations. This is, in fact, not so, since that identification itself will generate a dominance partial ordering (acknowledging an improvement in some achievement when it is unaccompanied by a reduction in any other). The relevance of dominance reasoning was discussed in the first lecture in general terms, and it is sufficient here to draw attention to the fact that an identification of objects of value without further valuation would nevertheless give us a partial measure of overall living standard. While that partial ranking will be silent on many comparisons – whenever there is a gain in one respect and a loss in another – the measure may still be of some considerable practical use. In comparing across class barriers, or in contrasting the living conditions of the rich with those of the very poor, or in assessing social change accompanied by progress (or regress) on all fronts, the dominance partial ordering may indeed give many unequivocal judgements of the ranking of overall living standard. There is no reason for us to spurn what we can get in this way, even when the finer aspects of relative weighting may not have been resolved.

However, there is, in general, good ground for wanting to go beyond this minimum articulation. The identification of objects of value is equivalent to asserting that these objects have *positive* weights without specifying what these weights exactly are. A sensible way to proceed from here is to confine the weights to certain ranges – possibly quite wide ranges – rather than opting for the overambitious programme of specifying an exact set of numerical weights. As the ranges of weights are narrowed, the partial ordering would get more and more extended. I have discussed elsewhere the mathematical properties of variable weights and partial orders, and will not go into that question here (Sen 1970).[13] But it is important to emphasise that the choice is not simply between no specification and complete specification of weights and that various intermediate possibilities exist and have much plausibility.

But no matter how narrow the weight specification is, the *source* of the weighting also admits some variations. Is the relevant valuation function that of the *person* whose standard of living is being assessed, or is it some general valuation function reflecting accepted 'standards' (e.g., those widely shared in the society)? The first point to note here is that these two general approaches, which we may respectively call 'self-evaluation' and 'standard-evaluation', both have some relevance of their own. Self-evaluation would tell us what the person would judge to be his standard of living in comparison with other positions (in line with his own valuations), whereas standard-evaluation places that person's living conditions in a general ranking in terms of some social standard (as it is reflected by commonly accepted values in the society). I don't think it makes sense to ask, without specifying the context of the enquiry, which of the two is, in general, the better approach. Which is superior must depend on what we are trying to compare and why.

The standard-evaluation approach has a good deal of use when we

[13] See also Basu (1979), Blackorby (1975) and Fine (1975).

are talking about, say, the extent of poverty in a community in terms of 'contemporary standards'. I have tried to discuss elsewhere the relevance of this type of comparison (Sen 1981: Chapters 2, 3, esp. 17–19). An interesting and important empirical study of poverty in terms of contemporary standards can be found in the recently published book by Joanna Mack and Stewart Lansley (1985).[14] In this work, contemporary standards regarding poverty have been determined on the basis of extensive questionnaires, yielding considerable uniformity of answers regarding the need for particular commodities and the related functionings.

The identification of the poor is an exercise in which the focus is on the *minimum* living conditions, but the same approach of using contemporary standards can, of course, be used to *rank* the overall living standards of different persons and groups. The essential feature of this general approach is the reliance on some uniformity of judgements (when such uniformity exists) on the respective importance of different objects of value. The standard-evaluation approach can be used in many different ways in studies of living standards.

The self-evaluation approach is concerned with each person's assessment of his or her *own* living standard *vis-à-vis* that of others.[15] A person can, of course, regard his standard of living to be higher than his neighbour's, even though in terms of general 'contemporary standards', his living standard would be judged to be lower. There is clearly no paradox here, since two different questions may easily receive two different answers. If the contemporary standards are widely shared (or would be widely shared after adequate reflection), then the two sets of answers may typically not diverge, and the self-evaluation approach would then tend to yield the same results as the standard-evaluation procedure.

VALUATIONAL ASPECTS

The valuation of objects in the assessment of the living standard raises many complex issues. I do not have the opportunity to pursue many of

---

[14] One of the broader conclusions of their study is that in terms of contemporary standards the identified minimum living conditions are not reached by five million adults and two-and-a-half million children in Britain, covering about a seventh of the total population. See also van Praag, Hagenaars and van Weeren (1982).
[15] For some interesting studies of self-evaluation, see Cantril (1965), van Praag (1968), Easterlin (1974), Simon (1974) and van Herwaarden, Kapteyn and van Praag (1977). See also Allardt (1981) and Erikson *et al.* (1984).

them here in detail, but I shall take the liberty of making a few brief remarks on some aspects of this problem.

First, the use of accepted social standards has both subjective and objective features. The approach might appear to be largely subjective in the sense that the building blocks of judgement are the opinions held in a particular community. But a deeper analysis of the problem would require us to go into the question as to *why* these opinions are held and these values cherished. Further (and more immediately), from the point of view of the social scientist studying contemporary standards, the opinions held are primarily matters of fact and do not call for the unleashing of one's own subjectivism into the problem of assessment. The balance of subjective and objective features is far too complex in an exercise of this kind to be sorted out rapidly here, but it is worth emphasising that despite the dependence on contemporary opinions the exercise has important objective features that can be neglected only at the cost of distorting its epistemological nature. I have tried to discuss these questions elsewhere and will not pursue them further here (Sen 1981: Chapters 2, 3; Sen 1983b).[16]

Second, self-evaluation must not be confused with the *utility* of the person in any of its interpretations of pleasure, or desire fulfilment, or choice, for, as was discussed in the first lecture, self-evaluation is quintessentially an *evaluative* exercise, which none of the interpretations of utility in itself is. The distinction is of particular importance in dealing with the point, often made by utilitarians, that any departure from utility-based evaluation must involve paternalism: 'Who are *you* to reject the person's own utility?' The problem is more complex than that, since the person's own evaluation may involve differences from his own utility rankings in the form of happiness, or desire, or choice. The issue of paternalism, when it does arise, must relate to the rejection of the person's *self-evaluation* (rather than of utility).

Third, the rejection of the Pareto Principle, which builds on the unanimity of utilities, need not – for the same reason – involve any paternalism at all. Indeed, the self-evaluation of the person's well-being or living standard can quite possibly indicate a course of action that is distinctly anti-Paretian, for the force of any dominance partial ordering is derivative from the relevance of the objects on which that partial ordering is based. If the relevance of the individual utilities is

16 See also James (1984).

called into question, the force of the Pareto Principle is correspondingly undermined for social action (see Sen 1970, 1979b, 1983c).

Fourth, in the evaluation of the living standard, there are many intermediate positions between a *complete* ordering of all alternatives and the dominance partial ordering, which may be very incomplete, of the valued functionings and capabilities. As was mentioned earlier, the relative weights may not be precisely determined, but fixed over wide ranges, yielding partial orderings more extensive than the dominance partial order, but short of a complete ordering. There is nothing particularly embarrassing in not being able to compare every pair of life styles in terms of living standard. The ambiguities in evaluation (even in identification of 'contemporary standards') may require us to be silent on some comparisons while being articulate on others. There is no great failure in the inability to babble.

Fifth, the overall ranking of living standard is only one way of seeing this evaluation. Sometimes the assessment of particular components of the standard of living may be of no less interest. If it turns out that there has been an improvement in, say, the standard of nourishment but a decline in the standard of being sheltered, that itself may be an interesting enough assessment, even when we are unable to decide whether 'altogether' this indicates an improvement or a deterioration. The passion for aggregation makes good sense in many contexts, but it can be futile or pointless in others. Indeed, the primary view of the living standard, as was argued earlier, is in terms of a collection of functionings and capabilities, with the overall ranking being the secondary view. The secondary view does have its uses, but it has no monopoly of usefulness. When we hear of variety, we need not invariably reach for our aggregator.

FUNCTIONINGS VERSUS INCOMES

The last point is of a certain amount of immediate practical relevance. When making empirical comparisons of living standard, the temptation to use such aggregate commodity-based measures as the GNP or the GDP is strong, partly because these measures seem nicely aggregated and conveniently complete. Everything, it may appear, counts in the GNP. The question, of course, is: everything in what space? Commodities, typically yes; functionings and living conditions, possibly not at all.

Still, the diverse commodity bundles may appear to be well

aggregated in the GNP measure through the use of observed prices, and this appeals to many of us over the ambiguities of dealing with a variety of functionings without any simple and immediate method of aggregation. But can this possibly make sense if our real concern is with living conditions and functionings? Why must we reject being vaguely right in favour of being precisely wrong? The conflict between relevance and simplicity of use, referred to earlier, is indeed a hard one in economic measurement and evaluation, but it is difficult to see why simplicity of use should have such priority over relevance.

As it happens, the more diverse characterisations of living standard, with various components separately presented, can be used in many practical exercises without great difficulty. Consider, for example, the much discussed subject of the comparison of China and India in terms of the enhancement of the living standard. The Chinese economy, we are told by the *World Development Report 1984* of the World Bank, has been having a growth rate of 5.0% per year of GNP per head between 1960 and 1982, while the corresponding Indian growth rate has been only 1.3%. This comparative picture would also seem to be consistent with the impression that people visiting the two countries tend to get. Thus, everything looks in order, and GNP seems like a sensible enough indicator.

But the comparative picture of GNP growth does not bear much scrutiny. In the same *World Development Report*, China's GNP per head is shown to be 19% higher than India's in 1982, and by extrapolating backwards at the respective rates of GNP growth, we would arrive at the astonishing conclusion that India's GNP per head had to be 54% higher than China's in 1960 for the two sets of GNP information to be internally consistent. This is, of course, just nonsense, since all accounts of GNP of that period suggest that India's and China's levels were comparable, and indeed Simon Kuznets estimated the Chinese 'product per capita' to be about 20% higher than India's around that period (in 1958 to be exact) (Kuznets 1966:360–1). The apparent precision of the GNP and GDP calculations has thus yielded nothing but a picture of confusion.

Happily, that is not much of a disaster if the opulence view of the living standard is rejected in favour of the view of functionings and living conditions. The Chinese achievement in the living standard is clearly higher than India's in terms of many of the more important functionings. In terms of life expectancy, the Chinese get 67 years, the Indians a miserable 55, according to one estimate (World Bank 1984:

Table 1), and lower still according to others. The Chinese have more than two-thirds literacy, while the Indians hover around a third (World Bank 1983: Table 1). It is this type of comparison that can tell us what has been happening in the achievement of the living standard in China *vis-à-vis* India, and even the fragmented information on the important functionings tells us more than the oddly precise picture of aggregated GNP. In so far as the Chinese have done worse in some respects than the Indians, for example in not being able to avoid a famine, there having been a major one in 1959–61 (see Ashton *et al.* 1984), or in not giving the citizens access to various sources of news and information, these too can be compared in terms of certain basic functionings (Sen 1983d). The main point is that the successes and failures in the standard of living are matters of living conditions and not of the gross picture of relative opulence that the GNP tries to capture in one real number.

To take another practical exercise, in looking at the prevalence of sex bias in poor economies like that of India, one gets rather little help from figures of family income and even of family consumption patterns, though Angus Deaton, John Muellbauer and others have skilfully got as much juice out of that as possible (Deaton and Muellbauer 1980, Deaton 1981). For one thing we do not know who within the family is exactly consuming how much (e.g., of food), and for another our main concern is not with commodity consumption but with functioning. It seems natural, then, to look at the comparative pictures of mortality, morbidity, undernourishment, etc., in assessing sex bias at this basic and elementary level.

As it happens, these data are also easier to obtain, and tell their stories eloquently. The picture that emerges in India is one of great disquiet: greater female mortality at most age groups (except in the immediate neo-natal phase and age groups beyond 35); a declining *ratio* of females to males in the total population; greater female morbidity in the results of health surveys; systematically less use of medical services by women *vis-à-vis* men, and by girls *vis-à-vis* boys; and signs of greater undernourishment among rural girls compared with rural boys living in the same village and sometimes in the same family (see, for example, Kynch and Sen 1983; Sen 1984a: Chapters 15, 16; Sen and Sengupta 1983; Gopalan 1984).

If sex bias in the living standard is our object of study, then it does seem to make good sense to look directly at the living conditions of the respective groups and to form a judgement, even when there are difficulties in constructing an aggregate index of sex bias. The constitutive plurality of the standard of living can be dealt with not only through formal aggregation, but also through simultaneous assessments of the different objects of value.

CAPABILITY AND FUNCTIONING

I have left one difficult general issue for discussion until almost the very end of this second lecture, and that is the question of the respective roles of capabilities and functionings in the assessment of living standard. A functioning is an achievement, whereas a capability is the ability to achieve. Functionings are, in a sense, more directly related to living conditions, since they *are* different aspects of living conditions. Capabilities, in contrast, are notions of freedom, in the positive sense: what real opportunities you have regarding the life you may lead.[17]

Given the close connection of functionings with actual living, it might seem reasonable to concentrate on functionings rather than capabilities in evaluating the living standard. I believe that this is, to a great extent, right. But it is not fully right. Capabilities have a direct role, too, since the idea of the living standard has an aspect that is not quite independent of the perspective of freedom. Suppose I can choose various styles of life – A, B, C and D – and I choose A. Consider now that the other styles of life – B, C and D – become unavailable to me, but I can still choose A. It might be said that my standard of living is unchanged, since A is what I would choose anyway. But it is not absurd to argue that there is some loss in my living standard in this reduction of freedom.

One way of putting this is to argue that the value of the living standard is given by the capability to lead various types of life, and while special importance is to be attached to the actual life style chosen, the availability of the other options has some value too. Another, perhaps more illuminating, way of seeing this question is to demand that the functionings be 'refined' to take note of the

---

[17] Note that the extent of freedom must not be judged only by the number of alternatives; it depends also on the goodness of the alternatives. To take a simple case, if the functioning bundle x is superior to bundle y, and y to z, then the capability set $\{x,z\}$ is superior to set $\{y,z\}$. Also, in an important sense, set $\{x\}$ is superior to set $\{y\}$. The argument involves the relevance of 'counterfactual' choice to freedom ('what would you choose given the choice over x and y?'). On this, see Sen (1985a, 1985b).

alternatives available. Choosing *A* when *B* is also available is a different 'refined' functioning, it can be argued, from choosing *A* when *B* is not.

An illustration may help to bring out the contrast. Consider two people both of whom are starving – one without any alternative (since she is very poor) and the other out of choice (since he is very religious in a particular style). In one sense their functioning achievements in terms of nourishment may be exactly similar – both are undernourished, and let us assume that they are so even to the same extent. But one is 'fasting' and the other is not. The religious faster is *choosing to starve*, whereas the poor starver is exercising no such choice over whether to starve or not. In the space of *refined* functionings, alternative opportunities could thus figure in the characterisation of functionings *themselves* (see Sen 1985a: Chapter 7; 1985b). The notion of capability is, then, partly reflected in the identification of the refined functionings.

In fact, the relations between functionings and capabilities are much more complex than they might at first appear. Living conditions are, in a sense, states of existence – being this or doing that. Functionings reflect the various aspects of such states, and the set of feasible functioning bundles is the capability of a person. But among the beings and doings are activities of choosing, and thus there is a simultaneous and two-way relationship between functionings and capabilities. It is, of course, true that once the functionings have been suitably richly characterised, then we can again ask the question: What alternative 'refined' functioning bundles are open to this person? But in the process of getting to that point, considerations of alternative functionings (and thus of capabilities) have already been taken on board.

The formal problems of characterisation, while interesting, are perhaps not ultimately very important, and what is really significant in all this is to accept the legitimacy of certain freedom-type considerations as part of the conditions of life.[18] Thus the capability approach, broadly defined, is not concerned only with checking what set of bundles of functionings one could choose from, but also with

---

[18] The importance of freedom in judging a person's life was sharply emphasised by Marx. His liberated society of the future would make it 'possible for me to do one thing to-day and another tomorrow, to hunt in the morning, fish in the afternoon, rear cattle in the evening, criticize after dinner, just as I have in mind, without ever becoming hunter, fisherman, shepherd or critic' (Marx and Engels 1947 [1846]:22).

seeing the functionings themselves in a suitably rich way as reflecting the relevant aspects of freedom. The constitutive plurality of the capability approach to the living standard has to take note of this as well.

A CONCLUDING REMARK

I must end here. I have tried to present a particular way of seeing the living standard and its assessment. I have argued against some approaches that are fairly widely used – including opulence and utility. I have contrasted assessment in terms of 'self-evaluation' and assessment by 'standard-evaluation'. I have also argued for the relevance of unaggregated characterisations of functionings and capabilities, and of partial orderings of aggregated assessments.

The scope for empirical use of this approach seems wide enough. This does not, of course, imply that all the refinements are easy to incorporate in empirical studies. The important first step is to be clear about the nature of the exercise – what it is and what it is not, what it demands and what does not much matter.

Walter Bagehot had once remarked that 'one of the greatest pains to human nature is the pain of a new idea'. Happily, this pain need not occur here. The living standard is an *old* idea, and I have tried to argue that the pioneers who considered the demands of the idea – Petty, Lavoisier, Lagrange, Smith, Marx, even Pigou, and others – did point towards the complex issues underlying the concept and its diverse relevance. The fact that we have also been frequently led up the garden path should not make us overlook the value of the leads we have got. There is, of course, a long way to go.

JOHN MUELLBAUER

Professor Sen on the Standard of Living

1 INTRODUCTION

It is a great honour to be asked to contribute to the discussion of Professor Sen's lectures on 'The Standard of Living'. The fact that I very largely agree with Sen's viewpoint made me wonder at first about how much scope there was for discussion. However, the subject is at the heart of economics and both Sen's analysis and his own applications have been so fruitful that the problem became one of where to end, not of where to begin.

Let me summarise at the risk of gross oversimplification what I see as Sen's essential points for a practising economist. Standard of living comparisons have traditionally been attempts to summarise a basket of commodities relative to a different basket in terms of a single ratio. – For example, basket A is x% better ('more opulent') than basket B. This is what Sen characterises as the 'opulence' view of the standard of living. Making several traditional simplifying assumptions, including an unchanged utility function, the opulence view is equivalent to a utility or satisfaction view of the standard of living.

Sen argues that really there is much more to the standard of living than that and questions both the opulence and the utility views. He argues that the links between goods and utility or satisfaction are quite complicated and that several distinctions are crucial to understanding it. I hope my schematic representation of these links in Figure 1 does not misrepresent his views.

The first point to make about Figure 1 is that Sen has severe doubts about utility as the ultimate definition of the living standard, whether utility is interpreted as pleasure or happiness, desire fulfilment or simply as the reflection of choice. He prefers to concentrate attention on two intermediate stages – functionings and capabilities – and the

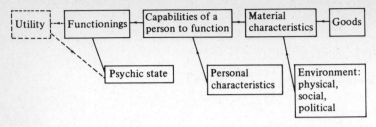

Figure 1. Utility, functionings, capabilities and their sources

dotted lines leading to utility in Figure 1 symbolise the weakness of the final link in the chain to utility.

The second point about Figure 1 is that Sen distinguishes three important links in the chain from goods to utility. Conventional market goods are first transformed into more fundamental intermediate goods, for example aspects of nutrition such as calories, proteins, etc. In common with some of the economic literature – Gorman (1956), Lancaster (1966) – he calls these 'characteristics'. These characteristics influence the capability of a person to function, for example to be well nourished, or to have a long life expectancy. These capabilities to function may translate in different ways for different people into the actual achievements, the functionings. Finally, higher utility is associated with higher levels of these functionings.

The third point about Figure 1 is that other factors apart from goods enter into the generation of utility. Starting on the right, we can see that the environment as well as market goods determines the amounts of material characteristics that can be achieved. The environment can include climate and public goods such as clean air, the absence of crime, and individual liberty. Secondly, personal characteristics, such as a person's metabolism, together with material characteristics, such as nutrition, together determine, in different dimensions, a person's capability to function. Next, a person's psychic state, as well as his or her capabilities to function, determine the levels of achievement in the different types of functioning. A person's psychic state might, for example, depend upon the possession of religious faith.

Although utility is at the end of the chain, Sen argues that the standard of living should not be judged by the utility level. In part, this seems to be because of the elusiveness of the concept. But even pinning it down and taking happiness to be the object of value would be too subjective and too quirky, since even for the same person the psychic state could be volatile. A similar argument can be made against taking the actual functionings achieved by the person as the objects of value. Instead, it is the set of available capabilities of a person to function which is, Sen argues, primarily what the standard of living ought to be about. And it is the multidimensional nature of this set which leads him to emphasise freedom, that is the feasibility of alternative options, rather than merely taking the chosen point in the set as a one-dimensional indicator of the standard of living. However, he recognises the practical difficulty in many cases of observing what the set of achievements might have been as opposed to the functionings that were actually achieved.

In the remainder of my remarks I shall discuss in Section 2 parallels and differences between Sen's arguments and related arguments that have been advanced by other economists. In Section 3, I consider the issues raised by habits, for whose existence there is much empirical evidence and about which economists have written extensively. Sections 2 and 3 aim to complement Sen's analysis and, by focusing on issues of observability and the link between behaviour and prefer-ences, attempt to illuminate both the advantages and difficulties he himself discusses. In this context, I also refer to the psychology literature. In Section 4, I venture some preliminary suggestions on the question of how the information entailed in a multidimensional capability set might be summarised. In Section 5, I respond to Sen's remarks about my work with Angus Deaton on the question of what if anything can be learnt about the living standard of a household and of the individuals in it from observing the market activities of the household as a unit. I suggest there is quite a lot of juice still to be extracted from studying the aggregate market behaviour of house-holds and that this could usefully complement Sen's work on sex bias against females in poor households. Section 6 summarises.

2 FURTHER ECONOMIC CONTEXT

The notion that market goods are not valued for themselves, but for the more fundamental sources of pleasure (and pain) they make possible goes back to Jeremy Bentham (1970: Chapter 5). Sen refers to Gorman and Lancaster as recent expositors of this notion that households produce more fundamental commodities or 'characteris-tics' from market goods. Characteristics here are features of a good.

However, this is a rather simplified view. Other writers on household production, such as Becker (1965), have stressed the importance of other inputs, particularly time and environmental ones, in the production of the fundamental utility-yielding commodities. In addition, by taking an intertemporal view, human capital is seen as an important input, though itself produced. Human capital is the label for any consumption sacrifice in one period that allows a level of consumption in a later period which is higher than would otherwise have been possible. Indeed, some of the writers in the Terleckyj (1976) collection regard health capital in a similar way as something that can be accumulated and may need maintenance, and would also acknowledge innate variations in genetic endowment.

In a sense one could say that for these writers the fundamental commodities produced by an individual or a household coincide with Sen's functionings, though for these writers the link from functionings to utility would typically be regarded as unproblematic. As in Sen, the fundamental commodities are produced from market goods, environmental inputs and personal characteristics which, as Figure 1 shows, are the sources of the capability set, that is the set of feasible functionings. Nevertheless, one can understand why Sen would not wish to identify himself too closely with this literature. In much of it, as in Michael and Becker (1973), rather restrictive assumptions are made (see Muellbauer (1974a) and Pollak and Wachter (1975)) which have the purpose of implying the existence of shadow prices which are the same for different households. From this follows the existence of 'as if' or implicit markets, on which the fundamental commodities produced by households are implicitly traded. This makes possible the extension of the discipline of the economics of the market place into the very interstices of household and individual decision-making. But it is important to recognise that, in itself, the household production view does not carry these implications.

Let me turn to the left side of Figure 1. Sen emphasises the variations in psychic states across individuals which can produce very different utility levels, or indeed different levels of functionings, from the same capability set. He carefully distinguishes variations in taste, that is in the shapes of the indifference curves held by individuals, from variations in the utility function. One might hope to deduce the former type of variation from observing the choices the individual makes. However, as Sen emphasises, two individuals, or the same individual at different times, may make identical choices when faced with the same capability set and yet may experience very different utility levels. It is this variation in subjective states which is one of his chief arguments against the utility view of the standard of living and for the view that it is the capability set with which a person is faced which determines the standard of living.

I would argue that it does not make a great deal of difference whether, as in Figure 1, the category of material characteristics is distinguished, or whether, as in a sophisticated household production view, the capability set (the set of feasible fundamental commodities) is directly determined by goods, environmental inputs and personal characteristics. What is important is that the relationships determining the capability set are relatively universal and that the determining variables and the chosen functionings are relatively observable. In particular, this means that the environmental inputs and the personal characteristics are relatively completely observed. If the latter, for example, are not, then the capability set will be subject to the kind of arbitrary variation that makes utility an unsatisfactory yardstick.

Operationally, the concern with functionings has a great deal of overlap with writings on human development in the development literature (see, for example, Ho (1982)), which have some of their roots in the 'basic needs' literature he discusses. This human development approach de-emphasises monetary economic indicators of achievement such as income or consumption, placing more weight on anthropometric measurement of physique and on health and morbidity, skills, educational levels and housing conditions. These are taken as indicators of achievement, but can also be personal characteristics and, if one takes an intertemporal view, can be inputs into future achievements.

It is interesting at this point to compare Sen's position with that of Stigler and Becker's well-known essay 'De gustibus non est disputandum' (1977). They argue that as far as possible one should assume that individuals share the same preferences for fundamental commodities. Thus differences in behaviour are not to be explained by taste differences but by differences in the constraints (the capability set in Sen's terminology). Thus they would explain the existence of individual habits or customs in terms of search costs associated with non-habitual behaviour and with the accumulation of specific human capital. For example, my addiction to mountains and my wife's to the sea-side is the result of different accumulations over the years of the

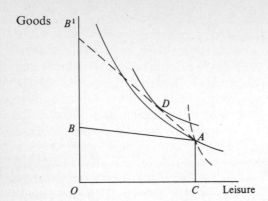

Figure 2. Consumption and leisure choices

kinds of human capital embodied respectively in skiing and swimming skills. Volatile fashions or fads that traditionally would have been regarded as examples of taste, they would explain through a fundamental commodity called social distinction which is produced from fashion goods bought by the household and diminished by those bought by other households.

Stigler and Becker are concerned with the explanations of behaviour rather than the determination of the standard of living. But they have put their finger on a fundamental problem common to both: what shall we attribute to the constraints households and individuals face and what to their tastes or utility functions? In this context, Sen criticises the practice of many economists to restrict relevant observations on the market choices of households or individuals.

One important area where asking people about their perception of the constraints they face is often the only way to make sense of their observed behaviour is in choices concerning formal and informal work and leisure. Clearly, the capability set would be judged to be rather different if a high level of leisure is enforced by the lack of work opportunity rather than freely chosen in the presence of work opportunities. The difference is illustrated in Figure 2. Suppose we observe someone with the consumption level CA and not working, that is at the point A. This could be someone faced with the opportunity set $OBAC$ and with the continuous indifference curves shown. With this opportunity set the only available work is at a very low wage – the real wage determines the slope of BA and, given the non-labour income CA, this person stays at home.[1] Had this person faced the opportunity set OB^1AC the point D would have been chosen and a considerable amount of paid labour supplied. On the other hand, someone faced with the latter opportunity set but preferences represented by the dotted indifference curve through A would still have chosen not to work. Artificially limiting oneself to just observing the levels of consumption and labour supply would make it very hard to tell these cases apart. Obviously, one would judge someone faced with the opportunity set OB^1AC to have a higher standard of living than someone faced with the set $OBAC$.

This example brings to mind a particular difficulty of interpretation which arises in Malaysia.[2] Part of the lower income of Muslim households compared with those of Chinese origin is caused by the lower levels of income contributed by Muslim wives. Given the cultural bias among Muslims against women working, the fact that very few of them engage in paid employment is not very surprising. But should one treat this as a difference from Chinese households in the taste for work or as a restriction on the opportunity set of Muslim households? On the first interpretation one would be much less likely to conclude that Muslim households were disadvantaged relative to Chinese ones. But perhaps the resolution of the difficulty is in raising another. If one drops the notion of unified household preferences, one would regard the cultural bias against Muslim women working as an aspect of the tastes of Muslim men but as a constraint on Muslim women. This switches some of the focus of concern away from differences between ethnic groups to differences within ethnic groups and indeed within households. It also raises some of the general questions about the economics of the family addressed in Sen (1983e) and to which I shall return in Section 5.

3 HABITS

There is a great deal of empirical evidence of the behavioural importance of habits. Sen touches only tangentially on habits and it is worth complementing his analysis by examining the difficulties habits pose for the conventional utility view of the living standard. However, these difficulties are not entirely avoided by his functionings.

---

[1] Leisure here measures time not spent in paid work and would thus include housework.

[2] I owe this example to Graham Pyatt.

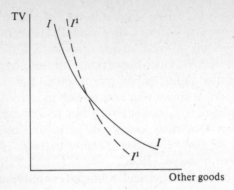

Figure 3. The effect of habituation

The effect of habituation to a particular good, in a simple example, say watching television, is shown in Figure 3. The indifference curve II is the one which applies when I watched a great deal of television last period; the dotted curve I^1I^1 is the one which applies when I watched little television last period. It indicates that the compensation in terms of other goods for giving up one hour of TV is larger the more TV I watched last period. My marginal utility from watching TV seems to be higher as a result of watching a great deal last period. Does this mean, however, that with the same budget and facing the same prices I am better off this period, having watched a lot of TV last period? Such a conclusion is quite unwarranted: the indifference curves cross and the inference cannot be drawn that one is better or worse than the other. However, one can deduce behaviour from Figure 3 by drawing in a budget line and finding the highest indifference curve which touches it. This suggests that the indifference curves corresponding to having watched a lot of TV last period result in more TV being watched this period. This positive feedback from past exposure is just the sort of behaviour which the notion of habituation would lead us to expect.

It is worth analysing this case a little further. Given diminishing marginal utility, a simple formal way of representing Figure 3 is to write the utility function as

$$u_t = U\left(q_{1t}\frac{(-a\,q_{1t-1}},{1-a}, q_{2t}\right) \tag{1}$$

where q_{1t} is the amount of TV watched in period t, q_{2t} is the consumption of other goods and a is a constant parameter. The case 0

$< a < 1$ corresponds to the case of habit formation under discussion while $-1 < a < 0$ would correspond to a durable good which yields services for one period beyond when it was new. If we are considering cable TV, which is paid for by inserting coins in a slot meter so that p_{1t} is the hourly charge in period t, the budget constraint is

$$x_t = p_{1t} q_{1t} + p_{2t} q_{2t} \tag{2}$$

It can also be written

$$x^*_t = p^*_{1t} q^*_{1t} + p_{2t} q_{2t} \tag{3}$$

where $x^*_t = x_t - a p_{1t} q_{1t-1}$, $q^*_{1t} = \dfrac{q_{1t} - a q_{1t-1}}{1-a}$

and $p^*_{1t} = p_{1t}(1-a)$

The demand functions which come from maximising (1) subject to (2) take the form

$$q^*_{1t} = g_1(x^*_t, p^*_{1t}, p_{2t}), \quad p_{2t} = g_2(x^*_t, p^*_{1t}, p_{2t}) \tag{4}$$

Thus

$$q_{1t} = a q_{1t-1} + g_1(x^*_t, p^*_{1t}, p_{2t}) \tag{5}$$

which, unless the budget elasticity of good 1 is too large,[3] means that there is a positive behavioural feedback mechanism. In other words, with a fixed budget and fixed prices, and starting with zero consumption of cable TV, my consumption builds up over time, eventually converging to a stable level.

One can build the effect of the durability of a good into the utility function in an analogous way and specify habits in more general ways. Since Stone and Rowe (1958), there have been many estimates of systems of demand functions in this general class (see Phlips (1983)).[4] The typical finding is that the habit-forming goods dominate.

Preferences such as (1) can be interpreted as follows: 'I consume quite a lot more than I did 20 years ago and feel comparatively better off than I did then (in fact similarly better off than if there had been no habit formation).[5] On the other hand, if I had to go back now to the

---

[3] 'Too large' means larger than $x^*_t / p^*_{1t} q^*_{1t}$.

[4] Incidentally, Spinnewyn (1981) has shown that it is fairly straightforward to derive such functions when consumers are forward looking and realise that building up a habit could make the good relatively expensive in the future. See also Muellbauer and Pashardes (1982).

[5] Note that if the rate of growth of consumption of good 1 is reasonably small $\dfrac{q_{1t} - a q_{1t-1}}{1-a} \approx q_{1t}$.

consumption levels I experienced 20 years ago I would feel a lot worse off even than I felt then. Conversely, if 20 years ago my consumption levels had overnight increased to my present standard, I would have felt hugely better off.' This seems unexceptionable. But there are two problems I wish to consider.

One is the problem of observability: what inferences can be drawn from behaviour? Any utility function of the form

$$u = \frac{H(q_{1t-1}, U(q_{1t} - a\, q_{1t-1}, q_{2t}))}{1 - a} \tag{6}$$

results in the same behaviour as utility function (1). Yet depending on how $H(\ )$ varies with the first argument, vastly different welfare conclusions could result. In the end some normalisation of (6), which may indeed be (1), has to be adopted, though asking people how they feel may well offer useful guidance in the selection of a plausible normalisation.

The second problem is one of how habits fit into Sen's framework. Are his functionings so fundamental that the levels attained in the past are irrelevant to the current satisfaction obtained from them? If so, habits characterise the 'technology' by which the functionings are produced, which is precisely the view of Stigler and Becker discussed above. I suspect Sen would sympathise with this position given his discussion of the case where satisfaction depends upon the consumption of others.

He cites with approval Adam Smith's reference to the capability to appear in public without shame. This capability clearly rests not on the absolute level of consumption or ownership of clothes but on the level relative to other people. I take it that the functionings of individuals depend on the consumption levels of others but not directly on the functionings of others.

The view that consumption matters not only absolutely but also relative to the consumption of other members of society can be nicely reconciled with the empirical evidence that Phlips and others interpret through the effect of habits. If there are lags in the perception of other people's consumption, then it is consumption relative to the past consumption of others that enters the utility function, and so the past consumption of others enters each person's demand functions. In the aggregate, therefore, past consumption appears in the aggregate demand functions even though there may be no habituation for individuals.[6]

One way of cutting through the difficulties in forging a link between behaviour and welfare is to ask people how well off they would feel facing different objective circumstances. Kapteyn and van Praag (1976), who have pursued this interesting approach, report that high-income people state a higher income at which their standard of living is satisfactory than do low-income people. This is consistent both with a habits view of utility and with the relative-to-other-people view if people tend to choose reference groups with a similar standard of living.

Psychologists, of course, have done a great deal of analysis of attitudes. They report surprisingly low correlations between indices of satisfaction and immediate objective circumstances such as income and health. However, there is wide agreement that indices of satisfaction are highly correlated with other attitudes, that these are quite stable over time and that they decompose into two clusters – E (extroversion), and N (neuroticism) – though different psychologists have different names for them.[7] To quote Costa and McCrae (1980):

Under the heading of E come sociability, warmth, involvement with people, social participation, and activity. Under N come such characteristics as ego strength, guilt proneness, anxiety, psychosomatic concerns, and worry. Extroverted traits contribute to one's positive enjoyment or satisfaction in life, although they do not generally appear to reduce the unpleasantness of adverse circumstances. Neurotic traits predispose one to suffer more acutely from one's misfortunes, but they do not necessarily diminish one's joy or pleasure.

I suspect that there may be as much disagreement among psychologists about the model of man and of woman that gives rise to such personality traits as there is among Cambridge economists about almost everything. Some would emphasise the role of genetics, others the role of the mother in early childhood, and others still cognitive distortions built up as a result of stresses in the individual's environment in childhood, at the time of transition to adulthood, and in adulthood itself. In my schematic Figure 1, I have listed psychic disposition as a contributory factor in explaining the levels of functionings achieved. By the very nature of the distinction between

---

[6] Kapteyn and Alessie (1985) have recently tried to distinguish habit effects from relative consumption effects on Dutch panel data. They find both to be significant but habit effects more so.

[7] I am grateful to David Clark for helpful advice on this literature.

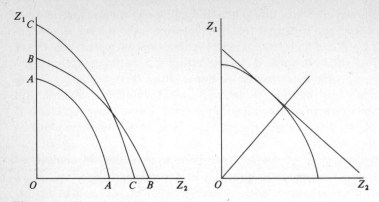

Figure 4a. Three capability sets
Figure 4b. Index number measures of a capability set

capabilities to function and the levels actually achieved, Sen is drawing attention to two problems. Not only may different individuals choose different combinations of functionings when faced with the same capability set, but they may also vary in efficiency: the achievements of some may be far from the frontier of the capability set. Potentially, a psychologist might be able to explain these variations, or perhaps characterise the information necessary to redefine the location of the capability set's frontiers.

4 SUMMARISING SETS

Sen emphasises the importance of freedom in determining the standard of living. Freedom means having a capability set that offers plenty of opportunity for choice.[8] He acknowledges that this raises questions about how to aggregate the multidimensional information that is entailed in describing an opportunity set and suggests that one might be satisfied with partial orderings, that is one might not be able to rank all possible sets. Figure 4(a) illustrates where Z_1 and Z_2 are levels of two functionings. The set OBB is obviously better than the set OAA but cannot be ranked with the set OCC.

Faced with the problem of ranking sets, the theory of economic index numbers would proceed in one of two ways. These are illustrated in Figure 4(b). The first is to consider the position of

---

[8] In Sen (1985b) he further refines the concept of freedom by distinguishing 'agency freedom' from 'well-being freedom'. The latter, which focuses on the capability set relevant for well-being, is what Section 4 discusses.

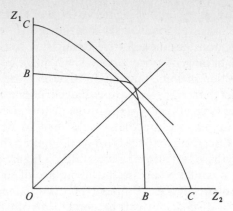

Figure 5. Opportunity sets and freedom

tangents to the frontier of the capability set. Having chosen a tangent of a given reference slope, the capability set can be compared on a ratio scale with others by measuring how far from the origin the tangent is. The second is to consider a ray through the origin. The length of the ray from the origin to its intersection with the frontier of the capability set then makes it possible to compare capability sets on a ratio scale. Applied to the problem of comparing sets OBB and OCC in Figure 4(a), each approach will come up with an answer, though the answer depends on the reference slope of the tangent or the ray through the origin.

It is clear that neither approach meets Sen's requirement that freedom should be an important issue in measuring the standard of living. For example, with the reference tangent or ray shown in Figure 5, set OCC is obviously worse than set OBB.[9] And yet one might well agree that set OCC offers more freedom – more opportunity for choice.

One approach is to summarise the sets not in one dimension but in a few dimensions; this would still economise on the vast amount of information needed to describe each set. The obvious way of doing so is to choose several reference values of the slopes of the tangent or ray; each value gives one measure of the set.

A somewhat more sophisticated approach borrows an idea from the measurement of inequality through a social welfare function.

---

[9] In the 'holidaying in Chernenkograd' example which Bernard Williams considers in his discussion, the set OBB would reduce further to just two points, which makes the issue even more stark.

Suppose there is some average or representative value of the tangent or ray slope. Using this gives a scalar set measure which ignores the diversity of the options desirable for freedom. Now consider a reference distribution of tangent or ray slopes which might be based on the actual distribution in some population. Consider the mathematical expectation of the scalar set measures that correspond to the different values of the tangent or ray slope in the distribution. This would obviously be a set measure that would tend to be more favourable to the OCC set relative to the OBB set in Figure 5 than the average tangent or ray-based set measures illustrated in Figure 5. And for the right reason: it would recognise the advantage of set OCC under a diverse range of preferences. Although this is a scalar measure that pays attention to diversity, it can be combined with the set measure based on the average or representative value of the tangent or ray slope to give a two-dimensional set summary. The ratio of the two can be regarded as an indicator of the diversity of options offered by the set. The indicator is somewhat analogous to the ratio of the equally distributed equivalent income to the mean income in the literature on inequality measurement.

5 INDIVIDUALS VS HOUSEHOLDS

Most households contain more than a single individual, and both the welfare and the behaviour of the individuals in the household interact. Obviously, larger households have larger requirements to enable their members to reach the same standard of living as members of smaller households. The question is how much larger, and the term used by economists to describe the answer is the 'equivalence scale'. This is the ratio of purchasing power needed by two households to reach the same living standard. But as Sen questions, do *households* have living standards? In Sen (1983e) he considers 'glued together' households, which act in a unified way, and 'despotic ' households, where one decision-taker imposes his will, and contrasts these with a more realistic approach where the individuals each have their own utility functions and collective decisions are the outcome of negotiation among the individuals. In the first two cases household utility functions exist which determine behaviour. In the third case no household utility function exists in general, though it will exist if there is a stable negotiated settlement resulting in stable relative values of the individuals' utility levels. But in every case one has room to doubt whether the standard of living of each individual is the same, for it is very hard to observe the consumption levels of individuals in households. On the other hand, individual morbidity and mortality data suggest that in some countries there exists a bias against female members of the household. Sen has himself done a great deal of important research on this question, which he discusses in his second lecture. Here he also comments: 'one gets rather little help from figures of family income and even of family consumption patterns, though Angus Deaton, John Muellbauer and others have skilfully got as much juice out of that as possible'. I would like to argue in response that we have not been quite as skilful as we might have been and I hope to do better in what follows.

I would like to discuss firstly whether the existence of inequalities within the household can be reconciled with the attempt to link welfare and behaviour in the equivalence scale literature. Secondly, I shall discuss what light, if any, empirical equivalence scale studies might throw on the existence of sex bias within households.

Three models for the estimation of equivalence scales have been applied. The first is due to Engel (1895) and takes the share of the budget spent on food as the welfare indicator. Thus the equivalence scale for a household with children is constructed by taking the budget x at which its foodshare is the same as that of a reference household, say without children with a reference budget x_0. Thus x/x_0 is the equivalence scale. The simplest way of rationalising this intuitively plausible procedure is to note that it is implied by a utility function

$$u = U(\frac{q_1}{m}, \frac{q_2}{m}) \tag{7}$$

where m increases with family size but is less crude than a mere head count, q_1 is food consumption and q_2 an index of non-food. For example, m would allow for the lesser needs of children compared with adults and could allow for economies of scale (see Deaton and Muellbauer (1980: Chapter 8) for further details). Note that in Sen's language we could think of q_{it}/m as a simplified type of functioning and m as the way personal characteristics, in this case household characteristics, affect the translation of goods into functionings.

The usual budget constraint can also be written in the form

$$\frac{x}{m} = p_1 \frac{q_1}{m} + p_2 \frac{q_2}{m} \tag{8}$$

At given prices the budget deflated by m is a monetary measure of the standard of living, and maximising (7) subject to (8) implies that the budget shares are functions of the budget thus deflated. Therefore, by observing how budget shares vary with the budget, the implied values of the deflators m can be deduced. This method is so simple that it can be used without any econometrics; it requires only graph paper.

A second method which is equally simple to use rests on rather different assumptions and is due to Rothbarth (1943) (see Deaton and Muellbauer (1986)). While in the exposition above the households' needs as measured by m alter in the same proportion for each commodity, in Rothbarth's model it is assumed that goods can be divided into two categories. One category consists of goods exclusively consumed by adults, with all other goods making up the second category. The idea here is that households with different numbers of children are at the same welfare level if their consumption of the goods not consumed by children is the same. Thus a household's equivalence scale is its budget relative to the reference household's budget at which the adult good's consumption is equalised. It can be shown that a utility function which leads to this model is

$$u = \min \{u_1(q_A, q_{B^a}), u_2(q_{B^c}, n)\} \tag{9}$$

where n is the number of children, q_A is the consumption of those goods exclusively consumed by adults, q_{B^a} is the consumption by adults of other goods and q_{B^c} is the consumption by children of other goods.[10]

Finally, adapting the third method, due to Barten (1964), to this A, B categorisation of goods, the utility function is

$$u = U(q_A, \frac{q_B}{m}) \tag{10}$$

This looks rather like (7) but assumes that only the need for those goods not exclusively consumed by adults alters as the number of children alters. As in the case of (7), we can interpret

$$\frac{q_B}{m}$$

as a simplified kind of functioning. Unlike (7), however, there is no simple graphical method of estimating this model.[11]

---

[10] (9) implies a cost function representation which is a member of the class Deaton and Muellbauer (1986) show is necessary and sufficient for the Rothbarth method.

[11] Indeed, in general m cannot be identified without price varying data or a prior parameter restriction.

Let us return to the question of individuals vs households. Suppose there are several individuals – an adult and one or more children, say. Let the adult have utility function $u^a = u(q_1{}^a, q_2{}^a)$ and each child have utility function

$$u^c = u(\frac{q_1{}^c}{b}, \frac{q_2{}^c}{b})$$

where $b < 1$ is a parameter and $q_1{}^a$ is the adult's consumption and $q_1{}^c$ the child's. Suppose that, taking into account the child's lower needs, the utilities are equalised and that the individuals each minimise the cost of reaching their respective utility levels. The compensated demand functions take the form

$$q_i{}^a = h_i(u^a, p_1, p_2), \; q_i{}^c = b \, h_i(u^c, p_1, p_2) \tag{11}$$

and $u^c = u^a$. Thus household demand functions with n children are

$$q_i = (1 + nb) \, h_i(u, p_1, p_2) \tag{12}$$

If Engel curves are linear but not necessarily through the origin, it can be shown that the case of equality $(u^a \neq u^c)$ implies exactly the same set of Engel curves as the case for inequality $(u^a \neq u^c)$. The intuition is that with linear Engel curves the degree of inequality does not matter as long as the total budget remains the same. One would then see no observable difference in household behaviour between two households with the same budget where the children are well treated in one and badly treated in the other. With non-linear Engel curves, for example of the type analysed in Muellbauer (1975), inequality does matter and there would be an observable difference. One might have thought, if (11) were the true model but $u^c \neq u^a$ and one estimated Engel curves corresponding to (12) instead, that one would find that a reduction in u^c/u^a would show up as a similar reduction of b in (12). But it is easy to construct plausible examples where a reduction in u^c/u^a leads to a rather smaller reduction in the implied b in (12).

This has disturbing implications for the use of the equivalence scale model to test, for example, the existence of sex bias. Common sense would seem to suggest that one should be able to detect bias against female children by estimating lower apparent needs, that is lower values of b, associated with them, compared with male children. But as the linear Engel curve case on the previous page shows, there might be such a sex bias and yet no detectable difference in household behaviour. And it is quite likely even with more plausible Engel curves, where an observable difference is predicted, that one would underestimate the degree of sex bias.[12]

The Rothbarth model (9) is much more favourable as a vehicle for testing the sex bias. The $u_i(\ )$ functions in (9) can be explicitly interpreted as adults' and children's utility functions. Reformulate (9) as

$$u = \min \{u_1(q_A, q_B{}^a), \frac{1}{k} u_2(q_B{}^c, n)\} \tag{13}$$

where, for example, $k = 1$ for male children and $k < 1$ for female children. In this model the evidence of sex bias would show up in the form of a higher consumption of adult goods in households with a preponderance of female children compared with households with the same total budget but a preponderance of male children. This is an easily testable proposition, though in practice the slightly lower body weight of female babies and children, even in wealthy societies with apparently little sex bias, would suggest the need for a lower food intake and so slightly lower overall requirements compared with male children.

Finally, the Barten model has the property that for the class of preferences which leads to the Linear Expenditure System of demand equations, no behavioural difference is observable as a result of a sex bias in the distribution of utility. For more realistic and general classes of preferences there *are* behavioural differences, but they are likely to be less easily detectable than with the Rothbarth approach.

The conclusion I draw from all this is that it would be too negative to conclude that equivalence scale models applied to the market behaviour of households can tell us nothing about the distribution of welfare within the household. In particular, the Rothbarth model is a suitable vehicle for testing for the existence of sex bias. Though it has been applied a number of times to estimating the cost of children since the original applications by Henderson (1949) and Nicholson (1949), most recently in the sophisticated study by Deaton, Ruiz-Castillo and Thomas (1985),[13] I am not aware of any applications of it to the investigation of sex bias within households.

[12] This may be the reason why Deaton (1981), who tests for behavioural differences by the sex of the children in Sri Lankan households, finds the difference insignificant. On the other hand, it may be that pronounced sex biases are absent in Sri Lanka.

[13] Incidentally, this study tests hypotheses regarding the appropriate list of goods to include in the adult goods set and finds that one can do much better than the traditional goods, drink and tobacco. Since consumption of the latter tends to be subject to measurement with considerable error, this overcomes an important potential objection to the technique.

6 CONCLUSIONS

I began by summarising what seem to me Sen's main conclusions. He views the standard of living as determined by the opportunity set of basic capabilities to function which a person has available. This capability set in turn is determined by goods, environmental factors and personal characteristics. Sen further argues that the freedom to choose, that is the extent of the opportunity set rather than merely the point in it that happens to be chosen, is an important ingredient of the standard of living.

In Section 2, I suggested that Sen's approach had much in common with parts of the literature on household production though not with those parts, based on highly simplified models, which analyse households largely in terms of uniform implicit markets. Sen's approach is also much in sympathy with the 'human development' strand of the development economics literature. Here 'non-economic' aspects of achievement, such as body size and function, educational levels, and morbidity, are emphasised. I also discussed some of the difficulties which arise in attributing variations in behaviour and living standards to variations in utility functions on the one hand, or to variations in external circumstances on the other. As another example of the difficulty of attributing choices and welfare to constraints or to preferences, I discussed a conundrum which arises in the context of work–leisure choice.

In Section 3, I considered some problems posed by habits and how habits fit into Sen's framework. I argued that the view that we are all creatures of habit did not in itself mean that utility has necessarily grown much more slowly with economic growth than real consumption has, as some economists have suggested. Such a view might more reasonably be justified by the assumption that some functionings are defined relative to those of others, an important aspect of Sen's definition of functionings. I also cited some research in psychology which may throw further light on the links between capabilities, functionings and satisfaction.

In Section 4, I ventured some preliminary suggestions inspired by Sen's comment that freedom is an important aspect of the standard of living. These were based on an integration of some ideas from the literature on economic index numbers and from the literature on inequality measurement.

Finally, Section 5 considered the relation between the individual and the household. It is hard to disagree with Sen's view that the individual is the ultimate focus of concern, and so with the implication that the distribution of the standard of living within the household is an important research topic. I examined what the literature on equivalence scales might have to contribute to this question, particularly to the investigation of sex bias within households. I concluded that one approach in particular, that due to Rothbarth, offered a promising line of enquiry which was likely to complement usefully the research that Sen had already done on this topic.

RAVI KANBUR*

The Standard of Living: Uncertainty, Inequality and Opportunity

1 INTRODUCTION

Upon the fairest prospects of earthly happiness,
attend uncertainty and mischance
Epitaph in Madingley church

If it is hard to think of an idea more immediate than that of the living standard, it must be equally hard to think of a phenomenon more pervasive than that of uncertainty. As Arrow (1971) has noted, almost every aspect of economic life, and life in general, is influenced by uncertainty. How, then, does the presence of uncertainty affect the conceptualisation of the standard of living? This is the question to which these comments are addressed. I am only able to touch upon a limited number of issues and will focus attention on some key points raised in Sen's lectures.

At the core of Sen's first lecture is a critique of utility-based views of the standard of living. In terms of what he calls the competitive plurality of views on the standard of living, the utility approach is clearly rejected by Sen. In his second lecture Sen goes on to develop an alternative line of argument whose culmination is the advocacy of what is termed the capability approach to the standard of living. However, as Sen is well aware, there are several issues that still have to be sorted out in terms of the constitutive plurality of this approach. As we shall see, uncertainty considerations impinge upon both the competitive and the constitutive plurality of views in the standard of living. In particular, it will be argued that while uncertainty strengthens much of Sen's critique of utility-based views, it raises and

*I am indebted to Amartya Sen for discussions and correspondence on these issues over the past few years.

highlights some tricky problems in the constitutive pluralism of the capabilities approach, problems which deserve serious attention.

2 THE SEN–WILLIAMS EXAMPLE

To focus ideas, consider the following example. There are two individuals, Sen and Williams (those who wish to stick to formal notation can think of these individuals as A and B, respectively), and a cake. Since I want to introduce uncertainty I will give them the option of either dividing the cake equally, or of tossing for the cake with a coin that is fair, and is known to be fair. What will Sen and Williams decide? I do not know, but I want the example set up so that both choose to toss for the cake rather than, for example, divide it equally, with the result that after the toss one person has all the cake and the other has none. Suppose (in deference to the Tanner Lecturer) that Sen wins and Williams loses.

There appears to be great inequality in the standard of living of the two agents *ex post*. Suppose our egalitarian sentiments are aroused and we move to equalise the cake distribution. What sorts of argument might Sen use to try to stem this egalitarianism? Of course, we know he will not use the argument that he is deeply miserable because he loathes and detests cake – the correct response to this is of course to tell him to give all of his cake to poor Williams, thereby making both of them better off while equalising the cake distribution. The argument Sen might try to get away with is that in fact he is less happy than Williams despite having more cake because he adores cake and would like to have his cake, eat it and have some more, whereas Williams does not appreciate the finer points of cake. But of course by now we have all read Sen's first lecture and know how to dispose of these utility-based arguments. The fact of the matter is, we tell him, that he has a higher standard of living than Williams – whether measured in terms of opulence or capabilities, since this is a society in which cake is the unit of account, medium of exchange and store of value – and that we wish to equalise that standard of living by taking all of his cake and giving it to Williams.

It is now that Sen turns to the argument of his second lecture: redistribution of cake after the event is akin to denying him the freedom to decide whether to toss for the cake or to divide it equally. By taking away the cake he won fair and square we may or may not reduce his standard of living *ex post*. But we certainly reduce his *ex ante* capabilities and, perhaps equally important, we reduce the *ex ante* capabilities of Williams as well by in effect nullifying his choice to gamble rather than play safe. It is of course interesting to speculate on how Williams might argue in defence of his and Sen's freedom to engage in lotteries of their choice *ex ante*, when faced with the prospect of having to choose whether to turn down the transfer of cake *ex post* or not! But by now the example has done its work in introducing the central issues, and it is time to move on to a more detailed analysis.

3 UNCERTAINTY AND THE UTILITY-BASED VIEW OF THE STANDARD OF LIVING

In his discussion of the claims of utility in the evaluation of the standard of living, Sen distinguishes between two possible uses of utility – as an object of value and as the method of valuation. Running across this are at least three different ways of defining utility – pleasure, desire fulfilment and choice. For each of the six resulting boxes Sen carries out a meticulous critique of the utility view. The links between utility, in any of the six versions, and the living standard are argued to be weak: 'they are second cousins rather than siblings'. How does the presence of uncertainty affect this assessment?

The theory of rational choice under uncertainty is by now well developed and I need not go into the details here. Suffice it to say that, under certain axioms (see Arrow (1971)), choice between lotteries is guided by the expected utility of each lottery – this expected utility being the sum of the utility of each outcome weighted by its probability. These axioms are not of course uncontroversial, but in what follows I shall assume that the 'expected utility theorem' holds (Machina (1982) shows that even if one of the more controversial axioms is violated, results akin to the expected utility theorem can still be derived, albeit only locally). The key issue that uncertainty raises is that of *ex ante* versus *ex post*: should the standard of living be evaluated *ex ante*, *ex post*, or some combination of the two?

If we take the *ex post* view, then the resolution of the lottery has taken place and the individual is faced with an actual outcome. What is his standard of living? It should be clear that Sen's critique of the utility-based view carries over straightforwardly to this situation. Utility as pleasure, or as desire fulfilment, can be argued to be an unsatisfactory reflector of the living standard, and indeed it was on these grounds that we turned down one of the arguments against redistributing cake in the Sen–Williams example. But the case of uncertainty highlights the weakness of choice as a reflector of well-being, *ex post*. Sen has rightly criticised the simple identification of the two as overlooking the complexities of motivation; it would, for example, be rather absurd to try and characterise the giving-up of one's life for a cause in terms of the maximisation of a utility function into which the cause enters as an argument. But there is a simpler and more direct criticism – choice is by definition *ex ante*. I may quite happily choose to take a risk, but be miserable once the (depressing) outcome is announced. The outcome was of course chosen, in probability, by choice of the lottery. The many–one correspondence between outcomes and action, a defining feature of choice under uncertainty, undermines the links between choice, utility and the living standard.

What of the *ex ante* position? Here again, if we were to treat expected utility as a utility, Sen's critique of utility as an appropriate evaluation of the standard of living would go through. Whether we think of expected utility as a mental state of pleasure (which Broome (1984) has argued against), or as desire fulfilment, or as choice, Sen's arguments would go through in terms of pleasure from the lotteries, the desire for lotteries, or the choice between lotteries. It would seem, then, that whether one takes the *ex ante* view or the *ex post* view, Sen's critique of a utility-based evaluation of the living standard either goes through straightforwardly, or is strengthened.

4 INEQUALITY: *EX ANTE* AND *EX POST*

Let us for the moment stay within the utility framework and let us moreover imagine Sen and Williams to be identical in every respect – except of course for the fact that after the toss Sen has the cake and Williams does not. Is there inequality in this Sen–Williams society? Of course, one response to this question would be to say that it is a non-question: there is equality *ex ante*, but inequality *ex post*. But it would be a pity if we accepted this response and let the matter rest there. Whether we like it or not, implicitly there will be attempts to weigh the two against each other and perhaps establish the primacy of one over the other. It could be argued, for example, that there is no cause for our egalitarian sentiments to be aroused at the sight of Sen with cake and Williams without, since *ex ante* they were equal.

A particularly powerful argument along these lines is put forward by Milton Friedman (1962) and, to be fair, his attempt to establish the primacy of the *ex ante* view is explicit rather than implicit. In the chapter on the 'Distribution of income', he leads off the argument with Adam Smith's principle of compensating differences – inequality of money income is often required to equalise utilities if, for example, some jobs are more attractive than others. Friedman extends this principle in an ingenious direction:

Another kind of inequality arising through the operation of the market is also required, in a somewhat more subtle sense, to produce equality of treatment, or to put it differently to satisfy men's tastes. It can be illustrated most simply by a lottery. Consider a group of individuals who initially have equal endowments and who agree voluntarily to enter a lottery with very unequal prizes. The resultant inequality of income is surely required to permit the individuals in question to make the most of their initial equality . . . Much of the inequality of income produced by payment in accordance with product reflects 'equalizing' differences or the satisfaction of men's taste for uncertainty.

It is of course an open question as to how much of observed inequality of income can be attributed to 'equality *ex ante*' (I have elsewhere investigated the relationship between the extent of risk-taking and the extent of inequality (Kanbur 1979)). But the thrust of Friedman's argument is clear – in the presence of risk-taking, observed inequality overestimates the need for intervention and redistribution. The Sen–Williams example is a pure case that sets out the issues sharply – *ex ante* equality versus *ex post* inequality. In this case Friedman would presumably argue that there was no case for intervention at all.

Let us set down the Sen–Williams example in the form of a table. The two equiprobable states of nature are Heads (H) and Tails (T). Action A is to nullify the effect of the toss by redistributing the cake equally, while action B is to let the results stand. I assume that H means a Sen win and T means a Williams win. The entries in parentheses show each person's utility under the different scenarios – Sen's utility is shown first, then Williams'. The same utility function is used to evaluate the cake allocation for Sen and Williams, both agents being assumed to be identical.

I would like to distinguish this example from Broome's (1984) Michael–Maggie example, which was originally put forward by Diamond (1967). In that example there is *ex post* inequality in every

Table 1. *The Sen–Williams example*

Actions	States of nature	
	H	T
A	$[U(1/2),U(1/2)]$	$[U(1/2),U(1/2)]$
B	$[U(1),U(0)]$	$[U(0),U(1)]$

outcome, but expected utility is more equal with one action than with another. In the Sen–Williams example expected utility is more equal under one action than under another. Broome's question was whether one should promote equality of expected utilities, given the degree of inequality in realised utilities. My question is whether one should promote equality of realised utilities, given the degree of inequality in expected utility. Friedman's answer to this question, in the context of the Sen–Williams example, would be no. I would like to argue that the answer is yes.

Before developing the argument further, however, we should consider one feature of the Sen–Williams example which might be thought to complicate matters somewhat: although the degree of inequality in expected utility is zero under both A and B, the common level of expected utility is higher under B than under A if $U(.)$ shows risk-loving, and indeed this must be so since both Sen and Williams chose to take the gamble rather than opt for the safety of equal division. In fact, *ex post* the sum of utilities is greater under B than under A, whichever of H or T occurs. Friedman's claim that B is to be preferred to A might use either of these two factors as justification. However, in the *ex post* case, while the sum of utilities is greater under B than under A the inequality of utilities is also greater – social preferences may well give greater weight to the sum rather than to the inequality (or they may not), but the point is that some weight should be given to the utility inequality *ex post* if we are at all egalitarian. Using the argument that B is to be preferred to A because expected utility (the same for both agents) is higher under B runs into Broome's (1984) counter that expected utility as such is intrinsically valueless; it is simply the mathematical expectation of utilities (which of course *are* intrinsically valuable). It can be a guide to the sum of utilities – whether this will be higher or lower – but it cannot be valued for itself.

In fact, if expected utility is intrinsically valueless, then equality of expected utility should exercise no special claim in judging between

If Shackle's argument is persuasive, and it must be admitted that more thought is needed in tidying up its edges and working out its consequences, then we do have a case for saying that *ex ante* and *ex post* are different animals: against the intuitive appeal of 'he knew what he was doing' can be pitted the intuitive appeal of 'tomorrow's hunger cannot be felt today'. To the extent that the latter has some force, a case can be made for redistributing cake from Sen to Williams. Of course, it is true that if this rule was known and appreciated universally, it would have incentive effects. So be it. We are all aware in other areas of economics that equality of cake distribution may have a cost in terms of the size of the cake. But that is no reason for not having equality as one of the objectives, and *ex ante* equality is certainly no reason for not having *ex post* equality as one of the objectives.

In terms of Table 1, the utility function that is used to represent the *perceived* utility consequences of the outcomes of the lottery before the event is not the same as the utility function that represents the *actual* utility of outcomes once they are known. Expected utility, using the *ex ante* utility function, can be used to *predict* behaviour but not to *evaluate* it. I realise, of course, that such a formulation sits uneasily with our formulation of rational choice, and I do not know how precisely to formalise the intuition that 'tomorrow's hunger cannot be felt today'. But Schelling (1984), for one, is well aware of the *ex ante/ex post* problem in the analysis of self-command and the rational consumer, and Williams (1981), in a different context, plays upon the distinction between *ex ante* and *ex post*. All I wish to argue here is that Shackle's argument has some weight and, the theory of rational choice notwithstanding, pushes us in the *ex post* direction in the Sen–Williams example.

5 CAPABILITIES AND FREEDOM: *EX ANTE* AND *EX POST*

As suggested in Section 2, faced with a thwarting of his utility-based counter to our egalitarian sentiments, Sen might try a different tack in leading us away from wanting to redistribute cake in favour of Williams. Following his second lecture, Sen might wish to argue that such redistribution reduces the standard of living of *both* Sen *and* Williams, since it in effect denies them the opportunity to engage in lotteries with unequal prizes. Now it will not surprise you that so far as mounting a defence of Sen's freedom to engage in lotteries is

the two actions A and B. If we look at the whole picture, then, of th
four factors characterising the comparison between B and A – n
inequality of expected utility in either, higher expected utility for botl
in B, greater inequality of utilities in B, higher sum of utilities in B
only the last two matter; in particular, equality of expected utility is n
reason for giving a zero or a much diminished weight to differences ir
the inequality of realised utilities.

Up to now I have essentially followed Broome's (1984) argumen
that the mathematical expectation of utility is not the same thing as
utility. Suppose it was. Then of course the foregoing argument could
not hold. There is a further defence of the *ex post* evaluation that
could be mounted, however. Much of the intuitive force behind
favouring the *ex ante* view lies in an argument that if individuals
'know what they are doing', they should be allowed to take the
consequences of their freely chosen actions. I will deal with the
question of freedom in the next section, but I now want to challenge
the intuition behind this argument by suggesting that it may not be
possible for individuals to fully know or appreciate the consequences
of their actions. This line of argument has been pursued by Shackle
(1965). In a passage that I think deserves to be better known, he
observes:

I do not think it is *necessarily possible in the nature of things* for information, as
it exists in the human mind (and that is its only real existence) to be perfect in
the sense that anticipative and retrospective utility would be bound to be the
same. Suppose I am a young man with a splendid fortune. I decide to pursue
all the joys of youth; I know that in doing so I shall dissipate my fortune, but I
am the 'prodigal son' of our Bible story of which you may know; when middle
age comes, I find myself destitute and filled with regret, regret which I *foresaw*.
Two moments, two *different* dates, cannot be the same moment, cannot give
to an event, an action, a situation, which objectively are one and the same
events or actions, the *same meaning* for the individual. I do not think, in
human terms, knowledge can be so perfect that tomorrow's hunger can be felt
today.

I confess that Shackle's argument, put forward in a comment on a
paper by Mukerji (1965) in a similar vein, appeals to me. It lies behind
the sympathy that I and most other people would feel for uninsured
flood victims, and why we would not feel strongly disposed to arguing
against government measures to help them, for example, by suggesting that the victims must now take the consequences of their
(underinsured) actions.

concerned, Milton Friedman got there first. In the same passage from which I quoted earlier, he argues: 'Redistribution of income after the event is equivalent to denying them the opportunity to enter the lottery'. He goes on to argue against redistributive taxation in this context because 'the taxes are imposed *after* it is already largely known who have drawn the prizes and who the blanks in the lottery of life, and the taxes are voted mostly by those who think they have drawn the blanks'. And lest it be thought that the Sen–Williams example is fanciful and irrelevant, Friedman comes not only to Sen's defence but to mine as well:

This case is far more important in practice than would appear by taking the notion of a 'lottery' literally. Individuals choose occupations, investments and the like partly in accordance with their tastes for uncertainty. The girl who tries to become a movie actress rather than a civil servant is deliberately choosing to enter a lottery, so is the individual who invests in penny uranium stocks rather than government bonds.

Sticking then to the Sen–Williams example, discarding the utility-based view and moving to a capability-based view, we ask whether Williams' standard of living is the same as Sen's, despite the fact that Sen has the cake and Williams does not? Once again, we must avoid the temptation of being satisfied with the assessment that *ex ante* it is but *ex post* it is not. There is a real problem to be faced and we must not avoid it. A different question which touches on the same issue is: Would Williams' standard of living be lower if he knew at the outset that there was effectively no chance of entering a lottery? Well, clearly one aspect of his capability, his freedom to choose between entering a lottery and not, has been reduced. But his *ex post* capability to survive without living on the cake line would be increased – with the lottery we know, and he knows, that there is indeed half a chance that he might end up a cake destitute.

So which is to be given greater value – the *ex ante* capability to restrict one's *ex post* capabilities, or the *ex post* capabilities themselves? Should Williams be allowed the freedom to choose a probability of living in shame on the cake line? I contend that our intuition once again turns on the extent to which we believe that Williams truly appreciates what it means to live a life of shame without cake in a society in which cake is all. If, following Shackle, we believe that tomorrow's shame cannot be felt today, then the case for restricting the capability to undertake such gambles is strengthened.

The appropriate focus of attention is what Sen and Williams in fact end up being – not what they could end up being. Outcome, not opportunity, is what is relevant if choice is based on inaccurate perception, and Shackle argues that this must be so *in the nature of things*.

6 CONSTITUTIVE PLURALITY AND DOMINANCE REASONING IN THE CAPABILITY-BASED VIEW

In his lectures Sen often uses what he terms 'dominance reasoning': if situation x has more of some object of value and less of any other than y, then x is said to dominate y. This dominance reasoning leads to a partial ordering of the space of alternatives and, as Sen notes, 'there is no reason for us to spurn what we can get in this way' in resolving the constitutive plurality of a particular view of the standard of living. But how much can we get in this way?

The importance of uncertainty, and of the Sen–Williams example, is that it highlights situations where the dominance reasoning fails with respect to the constitutive pluralism of the capability approach. It is inherent in the nature of the problem that permitting individuals to choose risks that could lead to disaster is bound to lead to disaster for one individual. The introduction of uncertainty raises this conflict, and it is then incumbent upon us to face the issue of the relative weights given to the different types of capability – dominance reasoning will not help.

7 CONCLUSION

Let me summarise. In these comments I have attempted to sketch out the consequences for Sen's arguments of the introduction of uncertainty. In terms of the competitive plurality of views on the standard of living, the presence of uncertainty strengthens somewhat Sen's critique of utility-based views. In terms of the constitutive plurality of capability-based views, uncertainty highlights the fact that choices between different types of capability or freedom *have* to be made – dominance reasoning will not come to the rescue.

The crucial factor that uncertainty introduces is the distinction between *ex ante* and *ex post*. Both in the utility-based approach and in the capability-based approach, the Sen–Williams example highlights the conflicts that can arise. I have argued for the primacy of the *ex post* situation for evaluative purposes, both along the lines of Broome and along the somewhat more unorthodox lines of Shackle. That individuals may not fully appreciate the consequences of their actions, that tomorrow's hunger cannot be felt today, sits uneasily with theories of rational choice. Indeed, it is not clear how to give it coherence in our present framework of decision theory. But I think the notion has intuitive substance, and I invite more fine-grained thought to provide the analytical foundations for it. Schelling (1984) would also, I feel, welcome such an exercise.

Returning, then, to the Sen–Williams example, we find that Williams would be glad to know that I would be in favour of taking some cake away from Sen and giving it to Williams, and I would not be much persuaded by arguments that such an arrangement would in fact lead to a catastrophic reduction in the standard of living of both.

KEITH HART

Commoditisation and the Standard of Living

INTRODUCTION

The substantive question I address is how living standards are affected by the rise of industrial or commercial society, a phenomenon I summarise in the ugly neologism 'commoditisation' (Hart 1982b). If we want to understand the evolution of commodity economy, we also have to be able to talk about what it is not. Everywhere people do some things for themselves (self-provisioning) and sell their goods or labour (commodities). Modern economy is thus an uneven process of commoditisation, where large shifts in the balance between commodity and non-commodity production are normal. This is not an absolute contrast between subsistence and the market, since all families in the world at present combine specialised acts of sale and purchase with the performance of relatively undifferentiated work in domestic units of consumption. Rather, it would be more appropriate to speak of shifts in emphasis towards greater or lesser reliance on the market.[1]

The standard of living is more easily conceptualised as a quantity when commodity production is seen to predominate in economic life. The early history of economic analysis rested on perceiving the scientific possibilities inherent in measuring the value of commodities; and much the same is true of economic orthodoxy today. The value of unpaid labour is more difficult to measure than that of commodities; and the standard of living is always made up of both, even if we restrict

---

[1] I am aware that this dualistic approach neglects a third category of economic activities, namely public provisioning of goods and services by means other than commodity exchange, but I choose not to complicate my argument with this problem for now.

ourselves to the narrowest definition of its content. It is misleading to evaluate the contribution of self-provisioning to living standards in terms of current commodity prices. Much of this paper will be taken up with assessing the fluctuations which are characteristic of relations between the two spheres.

This focus on commoditisation, when combined with an interest in the economic transformation of backward regions, makes me particularly open to the approach of the classical political economists, who were likewise preoccupied with the effects of commerce and industry on a society constituted partly according to alternative principles. Amartya Sen takes a very broad view of the problem which absorbed Petty, Smith and Marx, but goes much further than their theoretical limits. Echoing Keynes,[2] he asks 'Why must we reject being vaguely right in favour of being precisely wrong?', adding that what is simply usable need not be what is most relevant. The point is well taken. But the problem of measurement cannot easily be put aside. It was not by accident that William Petty was the polymath inventor of Political Arithmetick *and* the first systematic economist in England. The commercial and scientific revolutions of the seventeenth century (and, for that matter, those of Renaissance Italy or sixth- to fourth-century Athens) had an important common basis in the flowering of quantification made possible by market transactions on a large scale.[3] Marx abandoned totally the attempt to determine the use value of commodities, considering only exchange value to be quantitative and subject to social laws.[4] Adam Smith implies that needs are culturally relative, while dismissing as inappropriate a general tax on consumed commodities, on the grounds of its being an inevitable source of increased wage costs. But his overall concern is with production rather than consumption and with the social determination of levels of output which underlie differences in the wealth of nations. For Smith 'opulence' (the subject of Book III) is clearly the greatness of a country's produce, and the value of that

[2] Keynes speaks of those who 'following their intuitions, have preferred to see the truth obscurely and imperfectly rather than to maintain error, reached indeed with clearness and consistency and by easy logic but on hypotheses inappropriate to the facts' (1936:371).

[3] Weber (1978:63–211; 1981) makes much of the role of calculation in the rise of modern economy.

[4] See Marx (1887: Vol. 1, Chapter 1).

production is objectively measured as the commodities yielded by labour in aggregate.[5]

If the classical school stands for anything it is the notion that living standards are the aggregate effect of a society's productive efficiency. Moreover, commoditisation was seen to be intrinsically linked to these divergent trends in production. It may be that social conditions in the advanced capitalist nations make it appropriate to conceive of commodity production as opulence; but in this paper the position adopted is generally consistent with the theories and attitudes of the classical political economists. Underlying trends in labour productivity are thus taken to be the key to improvements in the standard of living; and these have historically depended on advances in the commercial division of labour. Sen's concept of the living standard is correctly hostile to the subjective posturings of the utilitarian tradition in neo-classical economics, although his examples, like theirs, regularly construct economic relations as individual motives and behaviour. Here, too, it will be assumed that subjectivism is a theoretical dead end, and examples will be drawn from historical societies. Economic analysis is most useful when it explicitly addresses the historical context which shapes the questions we ask and the moral judgements we make. If it is not firmly anchored in the particulars of the modern era, the standard of living debate is reduced to being just another branch of secular theology.

It is the practice of British social anthropologists to make their arguments through a sort of empirical exegesis. For those who prefer their ideas and facts in separate compartments, what follows may be confusing. The core of the paper is a comparison between West Africa and Britain. First I examine the effects of commerce on the living standards of grain farmers and herders who occupy the dry savanna region of West Africa widely known as the Sahel.[6] Then I discuss briefly the pluralism of economic life at the core of industrial capitalism, referring specifically to two British examples – the first

---

[5]   In modern usage, 'opulence' implies riches, even being fat. It seems a rather loaded term ('too much') for a scale of commodity-based wealth which is intended to embrace rich and poor alike.

[6]   Strictly speaking, the Sahel is the 'coast' of the Sahara desert where pastoralism is possible, but agriculture is not. In practice it refers to a group of mainly francophone countries which came to prominence in the 1970s as a result of widespread famine, and whose boundaries extend into the dry farming country of the savanna. My own field research in north-east Ghana is the basis for many of my observations. Sen has written an interesting account of the Sahelian famine (1981:113–29).

industrial proletariat of nineteenth-century Lancashire and the recent remarkable re-entry of women into the active labour force. The contrast between the British and the African cases can easily be represented as one between industrial and pre-industrial economies. In the one, a commodity economy is assumed to be pervasive, in the other, recent and contingent. Consequently our notions of the industrialised West are highly abstract and oversimplified, in keeping with the economic theories of both right and left, while ethnographic descriptions of African economies have been concrete and complex. My attempt to place the two on a common footing, for comparison's sake, necessarily emphasises the shared process of commoditisation in each. The discussion occupies a descriptive middle ground, more complex than Western economic models, more abstract than African ethnography.

THE WEST AFRICAN SAVANNA[7]

West Africa is divided roughly into two ecological zones – the wet tropical forest near the coast and the dry inland savanna which merges gradually with the Sahara desert. Although most coastal countries have savanna interiors, the latter zone consists mainly of Senegal and the Gambia, Mauritania, Mali, Bourkina Faso (Upper Volta), Niger, Chad and Northern Nigeria (whose population is as large as the rest put together). Population densities range from 2 per sq. km to 50–100 per sq. km in some pockets of intensive agricultural settlement. Cities are few, being in the main administrative centres and trading entrepots. The area's landlocked peoples make a living from the cultivation of cereals (millet and sorghum) during a short wet season. Livestock are raised as a source of food, manure and traction. Water is scarce, especially on the fringe of the Sahara (the Sahel); hence the importance of rivers, notably the Niger and the Senegal. Recently the region has suffered a well-publicised drought and famine.[8] Despite the modern growth of export production (mainly groundnuts and animals, with some cotton and rice), the savanna is still one of the poorest regions in the world. Official estimates of GNP per capita are $200–$400. The savanna is a major exporter of migrant labour to the

---

[7] See Hart (1982a:65–7) for a brief description of savanna agriculture and pastoralism.

[8] Copans (1975); Comité d'Information Sahel (1975); Dalby and Church (1973); Sen (1982: Chapter 8).

cities and forest farms of Southern Nigeria, Ghana and the Ivory Coast. Its culture is broadly speaking a blend of Islam and animism; literacy levels are very low. Yet the area was the location of West Africa's most developed pre-colonial states. Its patchwork of ethnic groups is in many places dominated by a sharp division of labour between agriculturalists and pastoralists. Trade has been pervasive in the region since ancient times; all rural populations have long had ready access to markets. Technology is extremely backward; indeed, with the exceptions of some irrigation and ox-ploughing in recent decades, farming is still largely a matter of hoeing. Transport has been improved greatly during this century, but, being mainly overland, it is difficult, expensive and slow. Over the last few years, development agencies have promoted the vision of West Africa's savanna as a potentially major exporter of meat and grain; but at present all its constituent nations are net importers of food.

The contrast between regions like West Africa and the Western industrial economies is great enough to persuade some observers to adopt radically different approaches to each.[9] In general, very poor rural communities are thought to be driven by 'subsistence' imperatives, whereas the members of industrial market economies are apparently motivated to calculate marginal utilities, maximise profits and the like. The position adopted here is that families everywhere combine commodities with the results of their own efforts at self-provisioning, but the balance between the two spheres and the character of their interaction differ sufficiently to warrant empirical investigation in *all* cases. In particular, the quantified abstractions of economic analysis may be better suited to some social conditions than others, but they can never be assumed to be absolutely applicable in some types of society nor for that matter wholly irrelevant to those typified by the West African savanna. I begin, therefore, with an ideal-typical contrast between industrial and pre-industrial economies, more to illustrate the range of possible conditions than to suggest the inevitable outcome of concrete investigations into countries like Britain or Mali.

In Western industrial societies reliance on the quantification of commodities consumed as an index of living standards is partly justified by the economic forms that have come to dominate our collective existence. Thus people are conventionally classified as

---

[9] Thus the 'substantivist' school of Polanyi and his followers (e.g., Bohannan and Dalton 1962) insist that societies lacking factor markets, especially in land and labour, are governed by economic principles alien to market logic.

producers and consumers. This reflects the separation of workplace and home in the normal experience of wage earners; we produce somewhere in order to consume somewhere else. The independence of each participant in the economic process is reified in the form of personal pay packets, while the isolation of households has reached the point where the majority of people now live in units of one or two persons only. The practice of paying for work by the hour, week or month makes the idea of regarding labour as a quantity intuitively plausible. Its output is often readily measured, and living standards may be summarised as the purchasing power of wages. At any rate the value of consumption can be assessed as the going price of equivalent goods in the market. These developments in the organisation of common livelihood are the substantive grounds for that scientific revolution in our thought which makes quantification indispensable to reliable knowledge. Economists' models are thus reasonable, if incomplete, approximations to real conditions in industrial capitalist economies, where human labour is sold for short periods in man-made environments and households depend on commodities for the bulk of their consumption.

Conditions in most pre-industrial societies appear in some respects to constitute the negation of this description. Here people consume a significant part of what they have produced. The patterns of ownership, co-operation and product distribution make the isolation of households inherently less feasible. The groundwork for identifying meaningful quantities of labour has not been laid by centuries of specialisation. Rather, the supply of labour and demand for its products are subject to a diffuse social organisation which is not easily distinguishable from the routines of everyday life. Production involves *living* objects and means of labour (plants, animals, land, water), so that productivity is only partly determined by the work men and women do.[10] Dependence on nature in turn ensures that the work of communities includes significant religious elements. The bulk of subsistence goods rarely takes the form of commodities and this makes the various branches of consumption incommensurable. Under such circumstances, the technical difficulties of applying economists' procedures are formidable, rendering most efforts to do so fruitless.

West African social realities do not conform to either extreme type, although their villages come closer to the second than the first. A

[10] Much of this passage is derived from Hart and Sperling (1983), which is focused on the herding economies of East Africa.

world of export-cropping, taxation, schools and wage labour has been incorporated piecemeal into the more customary world of ancestor worship, granaries, family herds and polygamy. So, whenever a community makes a significant shift towards production for sale, there is likely to be some pressure to change the organisation of time. Activities which were relatively undifferentiated before become identified as separate forms of labour, each with a market price. Thus childcare and socialisation may have been casually intermeshed with the ordinary web of daily life, but the introduction of schooling makes them educational services that have to be paid for – by taxes or fees. West African agriculture is constrained by marked seasonal fluctuation of climate, so that for eight months rainfall is inadequate to sustain the farming of basic cereals. For this reason, as well as because of low average population densities and a low level of surplus extraction through rent or taxation, West African savanna dwellers spend rather less man hours per year on acquiring their food than most Asians, for example.[11] Yet, by our standards, they appear to spend an extraordinary amount of time on funerals. We are certain that growing plants is a better way of securing a minimal living standard than is servicing the needs of the dead. A West African farmer, faced everywhere by evidence of a hostile nature, looks to propitiation of the ancestors as an important aspect of farm-management. But the commercialisation of agriculture necessarily transforms evaluations of time; the results of specialised labour are increasingly realised as purchasing power. Then, attending funerals can be portrayed as wasteful – of time, money and energy – that trinity of standards by which modern societies measure efficiency and value.[12] Broadly speaking, then, if time is organised differently in industrial and pre-industrial economies, the transition between the

[11] Cleave (1974:34). Sahlins' celebrated account (1972) of 'primitive affluence' suggests that the dominance of domestic organisation in village agriculture establishes cultural pressures towards underproduction, including a tendency to work short hours. My point relates rather to the effects of a diffuse organisation of time on calculations of the inputs and outputs of specialised tasks.

[12] Sophisticated measurement requires continuous variables to be embedded in social organisation. Time, money and energy are three such variables permitting ready quantification in our society. It has been remarked that, if air transport had made the same technical progress as computers since the Second World War, we would now be able to travel around the globe in two hours for $50 on five gallons of fuel. Time, money and energy appear here as discrete quantities of obvious institutional relevance. But imagine how that idea might be translated into the idioms of a West African herder, who measures an animal's life span in years (if at all), pays no money to graze it and has no way at all of calculating rates of energy conversion (nor any conceivable interest in such a possibility).

two, however partial, is bound to be difficult. We know well how the early industrial working class was socialised to operate within the time discipline of capitalist factories.[13] We understand less well how our own intellectual endeavours in the Third World, especially those of economists, are often an attempt to impose the *quadrillage*[14] of modern discipline on the incoherent and largely pre-industrial economies of that region. The problem is not mental; it lies in the institutional contrasts that shape language. Before we talk of living standards in West Africa, we should consider the applicability of commoditised economic models to circumstances there.

The logic of the industrial–pre-industrial dualism leads readily to the assertion that one way of life cannot be evaluated by the standards of another, that the value of two distinct patterns of work and consumption is incommensurable. But the intellectual drawbacks of such an anthropological relativism are often as vitiating as the blithe reductionism of the economists. So let us first consider the attempt to measure movements in income level as an index of material deprivation and social well-being in societies such as those of the West African savanna, societies which have been involved in significant commercial developments during this century, while remaining weakly commoditised by international standards. Sen mentions some of the legitimate criticisms that can be made of GNP measures as an index of living standards. In the West African savanna many important goods and services rarely enter the market as commodities. The housing stock, for example, comes almost entirely from unpaid labour. Walking replaces urban transport fares for quite long journeys. Much food is never sold. Significant exchanges take place on a non-market basis – grain for milk, cows for marriageable women. Undoubtedly this low level of commoditisation in some important sectors means that national income measures are even more meagre than real living standards would justify. And, when markets expand – as they have in recent decades for foodstuffs, clothing, tools, local beer, imported luxuries and much else – the institutional shift in distribution appears as an often imaginary economic growth.

West Africans, like everyone else, do some things for themselves and buy other things in the form of commodities.[15] Sometimes the

---

[13] Thompson (1968); Marx (1887: Vol. 1, Chapter 15).
[14] The significance of 'organisation by squares' for early industrial society is explored by Foucault (1977).
[15] The arguments of this and subsequent paragraphs are expanded in Hart (1982a:126–35).

same goods may be either sold in the market or retained for purposes of self-provisioning. Thus herders may keep their cows for milk or sell them for meat. Even when domestic consumption is the exclusive goal of production, the existence of a market for those goods elsewhere suggests a measurable equivalence between the two. When commodity and non-commodity production are concretely linked in this way, it does seem inherently plausible to value consumption outside the market in terms of equivalent commodities. Thus, if we know that most grain farmers sell half their millet and keep the other half for family use, total millet consumption could be valued at twice aggregate market sales. And this is indeed the normal practice of national income accountants and of most economists concerned with rural incomes in the Third World.[16] But there are pitfalls even in this apparently simple procedure. Let us assume that household heads frequently face the option of withholding subsistence crops from the market or selling them at the going price. Clearly the level of commoditisation is a major determinant of market price in the first place. If most farmers withhold their grain from the market at one point in time, the price of what is sold will usually be higher than at some time when they rush to sell their whole crop.

The case is well illustrated by exchange between grain farmers and herders.[17] In normal times pastoralists hoard their cattle in order to build up their herds against future losses; they sell just as much milk and animals as they need to buy cereals, which are quite cheap because West African governments import a lot of grain from North America and South-East Asia, with depressive consequences for local food prices. The exchange value of pastoral products under these circumstances is relatively high, and the widespread use of cattle as bridewealth in agricultural communities acts as an institutional pressure that keeps prices high. But periodic drought forces the herders to sell more animals than they would like. Demand from the farming population does not rise equally; indeed, they, too, may be suffering from the drought. So a glut of animals on the market drives their price through the floor. Herders need more grain to compensate for the loss of pastoral products and cereal prices rise temporarily. But since food is now generally scarce, grain farmers are induced to hold

[16] A particularly sensitive critique of this issue may be found in Frankel (1953).
[17] The symbiosis between agriculturalists and pastoralists in the semi-arid zones of Africa and elsewhere is well illustrated by Khazanov (1984); Gallais (1972); and Sen (1981:113–29).

on to their most reliable source of supply, if they can. Their hoarding of grain pushes the market price up further. Swings on this scale are endemic to the West African savanna economies over time periods ranging from the short to the long run. The estimated total value of a farmer's income would thus appear to be higher if the level of commoditisation is low, as long as current market prices are used to quantify the value of subsistence production.

This point may be generalised to the ideal contrast between industrial and pre-industrial economies. In West Africa rural markets are the outcome of a number of forces including the world food trade, government pricing policy favouring the cities, merchant monopsonies and much else. But they are also significantly the outcome of forces generated within the sector of production for livelihood, which in many cases may be relatively indifferent to commodity prices. In industrial economies, however, as we will see, something like the reverse case may hold. Here a continuing process of commoditisation, fuelled by the progressive cheapening of goods available in the market, puts pressure on the domestic sphere to replace unpaid labour with wages and commodity substitutes. In any case, if we wish to understand trends in living standards, study of the determinants of these swings in the balance between self-provisioning and reliance on commodities offers more scope than short-run empirical assessments based on market prices as such. Moreover, it should be obvious that straightforward use of current commodity prices to evaluate non-market production is misleading or worse.

The rural savanna is the poorest segment of West Africa's highly uneven income distribution, and the regional average GNP per capita of a dollar a day indicates a level of poverty that no accountant's juggling can disguise. At the core of this phenomenon is the fragmentation and stagnant productivity of West African agriculture.[18] The classical political economists were convinced that expansion of the commercial division of labour was a necessary condition for substantial improvements in labour productivity, which in turn guaranteed increases in national wealth. Modern economists have abstracted from this argument only the concern with market growth, to the detriment of an effective understanding of Third World development. A thoroughgoing classical approach to living standards might focus on the 'socially necessary labour time' required for a

[18] See Hart (1982a: Chapters 1, 2, 7).

community's productive tasks.[19] To take one example, water is essential to human life and it is regularly bought and sold in industrial economies. How can we give a price to the task of carrying water in the West African savanna? It is an extremely onerous feature of village women's daily routine, involving perhaps a five-mile walk to a muddy pool in the dry season. No one could make a living being paid to do it for them, whereas in the region's cities workers often pay carriers to bring water for their baths, cooking and drinking (allowing us to cost the activity on a man/hour basis, if we so choose). Is such a comparison relevant to estimating village living standards? Obviously the women would be no better off if the price of water went up in the cities. When people do most things for themselves, what matters is a reduction in the labour time necessary for their various tasks. A year-round standpipe in each village would free rural women from a lot of walking. That would surely constitute a real improvement in their living standards; and it would reflect a *reduction* in the social cost of providing water. They might choose to use the extra time gossiping at the standpipe or working as part-time wage labour on a new cotton farm. In contrast to labour time indicators, calculations of the market value of subsistence activities measure mainly the level of labour specialisation and the demand for commodities, not relative living standards as such.

As a result of commoditisation so far, West Africans probably now work harder and have access to a wider range of goods and services. It is difficult to judge the costs and benefits of such developments. Unfortunately their average standard of living is low enough for the issue of physical survival to be relevant. Famines in the Sahel since the late 1960s have received as much publicity as those in Ethiopia and Bangladesh.[20] It is therefore appropriate to assess patterns of production, distribution and consumption in terms of their effectiveness in dealing with the hazards of the material environment. At the centre of the modern debate on this issue lies the question of the role of markets in promoting or undermining the security of marginal populations. It makes a tremendous difference to policy if you believe

---

[19] The expression is Marx's (1887: Chapter 1), but the sentiment is shared by his Anglo-Scottish predecessors in political economy; see Dobb (1973). The time taken empirically by individuals to perform a given task is different from the standard set by the prevailing level of technology and skills ('socially necessary labour time'), which alone determines the exchange value of commodities, if not their fluctuating price.

[20] See note 8 above; see also Swift (1977) for a review of the early literature.

that savanna farmers and herders would be better off (i.e., live longer) with *more* or with *less* involvement in markets. Sen's analysis of the Sahelian famine places primary emphasis on the adverse effects of commoditisation: 'while commercialisation may have opened up new economic opportunities, it has also tended to increase the vulnerability of the Sahel populations' (1981:126–7).[21] Which is the greater source of vulnerability – the dependence of locally insulated communities on unpredictable environments or the unseen vagaries of markets? It is like asking which is worse – exposure to barbaric warfare or life under the nuclear threat. But for Adam Smith and his successors markets promoted security by improving distribution and advancing productivity through division of labour. We may now know better. In the West African case, however, there is one disconcerting piece of evidence which might allow us to cut through the rhetorical oppositions.

The West African population has roughly quadrupled since the turn of the century – from under 40m. then to over 150m. today.[22] Birth rates have remained high, while death rates have fallen sharply – from 30 to 20 per thousand in the last two decades alone. Average life expectancy at birth has improved by 5–9 years since 1960, but it is still some 25 years lower than the norm for industrialised countries; and at 42 years in the savanna, life expectancy at birth there is 5 years below that of the West African coastal countries and 12 years lower than the average for the Third World as a whole.[23] Demography is a crude index of improvements in well-being, but it is a powerful one, especially for populations still exposed to pre-industrial conditions which have been virtually eliminated in many other areas of the world. To watch a 40-year-old woman mourn the loss of her twelfth consecutive child is to be forcibly reminded of the priority to be given to reducing this degree of vulnerability to death before other criteria of the living standard are brought into play. The shocking scenes of

---

[21] In this he was undoubtedly influenced by French Marxist commentaries on the famine, such as the Comité d'Information Sahel (1975). But the notion that involvement in markets increases the risk of destitution is intrinsic to his analysis of other cases in the book.

[22] These figures are even more suspect than usual, owing to incomplete coverage around 1900 and extravagant manipulation of the Nigerian census results in modern times. Recent figures on birth and death rates are more reliable, indicating at least a 3% per annum net increase in most national populations today or a doubling of the total since decolonisation a quarter of a century ago.

[23] These figures are taken from World Bank (1983).

starvation shown to Western television audiences are the *normal* conditions which keep average life expectancy in the low 40s and kept it much lower everywhere before the industrial age, when there were periodic gluts of death allied to chronic economic backwardness.[24] Forces like this must have kept back the West African population to a similar low level prior to colonisation. And, however bad it may look to us, life in the present-day savanna must be in some significant respects more benign than it once was, for it is only in this century, and particularly since the Second World War, that its Malthusian shackles have been broken. Whatever the contradiction of modern political and economic developments there, it has to be noted that these have been associated with a lot less death in the West African savanna. Nor is an absolute increase in numbers a threat, since the relative abundance of land and scarcity of labour[25] makes this population growth a positive factor in the region's economic prospects.

Few of the twentieth century's detractors would deny that it has seen the formation of powerful states linked to global commerce, in West Africa as elsewhere, during both the colonial and the post-colonial periods. If greater reliance on markets (commoditisation) is a major aspect of the region's modern economic history, it would seem that the overall consequences for material welfare have been on balance beneficial. What other interpretation can be placed on a quadrupling of population size in a matter of decades? To claim that the vagaries of rainfall have been aggravated by commercialisation seems to be rather perverse. Indeed it is more plausible to suggest, following Adam Smith, that markets, transport and modern states have improved life chances in the West African savanna than it is to suggest the opposite. The fact that the post-war period in particular has seen both the greatest expansion of trade and the most dramatic reductions in death rates tends to support this view. There is no substitute for a long-run historical perspective on these matters; otherwise we are free to indulge our various prejudices when making selective judgements about causation.

In the 150 years since West Africa was first drawn into world markets dominated by industrialising countries, the region has been afflicted by depression several times, notably in the late nineteenth century, the 1930s and most of the last decade.[26] The boom–bust cycle

---

[24] McNeill (1976); Cipolla (1978); McKeown (1976).
[25] Jack Goody (1971), for example, has made much of this contrast between Africa and Eurasia.
[26] Hart (1982a:84–5, 124, 134).

of world markets may have surprised savanna herders and farmers the first time, but not the second and even less the third. The severity of market swings is better known to these producers than it is to the latest crop of Western experts who have never experienced depression at first hand. Indeed West Africans have often been accused of an irrational conservatism during times of commercial boom for holding on to their livestock and grain stores rather than sell at relatively high prices.[27] My contention is that repeated exposure to the boom–bust cycle leads to a built-in flexibility of adjustment between reliance on commodities and on self-provisioning, an adaptive response which is likely to be less volatile than market price movements in the short term. This is crucial to any attempt to maintain or improve living standards. For example, a growing commitment to export crops or wages should not preclude a retrenchment onto subsistence farming when the market for goods and labour collapses. Massive fluctuations in demand for what they sell have been normal for West Africans during this century. The Great Depression was a decisive lesson for those who cut themselves off prematurely from traditional agriculture. No doubt similar lessons are being learned in the present economic crisis. The characteristic West African response has been to maintain a flexible mix of livelihood options. Post-war urbanisation on a grand scale has been based on a pattern of labour circulation between countryside and city which allows migrants to derive, from their membership of rural communities, a measure of security against dependence on the market.[28] For land is still quite plentiful and property in it has been retained largely by traditional groups. Commerce has been adapted to the needs of these groups. The day is still far ahead when indigenous economic strategies are shaped by short-run considerations of market price.[29]

One inference to be drawn from this analysis is that any precise weighting of the value of commodities and of self-provisioning in West African living standards must be fraught with difficulty, even if we do not conclude that the two are incommensurable. Sen's discussion of the 'functionings and capabilities' approach suggests a

[27] Herders in particular have been vilified all over Africa for what has been referred to derogatorily as 'the cattle complex': reasonable insurance mechanisms seen as an unnatural attachment by tribesmen to their animals. Khazanov (1984) summarises the literature.

[28] Gugler and Flanagan (1978); Hart (1982a:121–5).

[29] In the neighbouring forest areas, West African cocoa producers demonstrated their preference for the stable prices introduced by marketing boards after 1945 by substantially raising levels of output. See Bauer (1954); and Hill (1963).

number of alternative yardsticks for measuring trends in poverty. Sociologists have always emphasised the powerlessness of the poor, which is perhaps the negative reciprocal of Sen's notion of capability. Freedom from drudgery, reduced exposure to the risk of death, an expanded range of active choice open to individuals – all of these may ultimately be more crucial to living standards than commodity-based indices of material consumption. They are not, however, particularly easy to measure. Perhaps a focus on labour productivity (a sort of Taylorism writ large) offers a compromise between the usability of commodities and the relevance of capabilities. This is so for several reasons, principally because labour time offers a universal standard of measurement and because uneven developments in labour efficiency are the main source of the income gap between rich and poor nations. In the West African case it has been calculated that savanna farmers spend on average about 1,000 hours a year securing their food supply, whereas the paddy farmers of Indo-China enjoy a less varied and nutritious diet from 3,000 hours of work.[30] Yet casual observation would lead one to judge South-East Asia the more efficient economy, while West Africa is regularly portrayed as a basket case, with some justification. We need more counterintuitive facts of this kind as a stimulus to a fundamental reappraisal of our theoretical basis for making comparative judgements. How much labour does it take to produce basic needs – for food, clothing, light, housing, childcare, medicine and so on? What matters in the long run is not whether basic needs are met, but how much time is left over for discretionary activities (including further labour specialisation) when they have been met.[31] Such measures of time allocation would have to be relative to the priorities of the specific populations being monitored; and it is as well to remember that daily life in a village is organised on rather more diffuse principles than Taylor's shop floor.[32]

In this discussion of West African living standards I have fallen back on a package emphasising, at least initially, commodities, labour time and death. This is, of course, the perspective of classical political economy, enshrined in Malthus' *Essay on Population* as much as in the *Wealth of Nations* or *Capital*. The main virtue of the old economic

[30] Cleave (1974:34).
[31] See the discussion of water-carrying above.
[32] Anthropologists have recently shown much interest in time allocation studies, including the question of whether industrialisation reduces the time costs of production when domestic labour is included. See Minge-Klevana (1980) for a review.

theory is that it addressed gross long-run discrepancies in productive performance, not short-term marginal increments of value. The West African savanna has made some gains from twentieth-century commerce, but the area has made scant progress towards the goal of industrial transformation.[33] It remains trapped in a kind of dependency on the international economy which encourages both old and new forms of risk aversion to flourish. Consequently, commodity production and self-provisioning persist in a flexible and intimate symbiosis, and progress towards greater specialisation and efficiency of labour is inhibited. What is needed, especially, is an agricultural revolution capable of pushing the region's economies across the invisible barrier that marks admission to the ever-growing club of industrial nations. In its absence West African commercialisation will remain tied to stagnant production. Markets have existed in most of the social formations known to history; what is determinant of trends in production is the character of the dominant social structure, not the existence of markets as such. The societies of West Africa's savanna have successfully incorporated modern commerce into their functioning. As a result the prospects for advances in production are small, but the people retain control of the bulk of their productive and distributive organisation. Commoditisation is now intrinsic to domestic life everywhere, yet markets are subject to the forces of an essentially conservative social organisation. Death rates have fallen, but the region is still abysmally poor. The savanna economies are chronically vulnerable to the boom–bust cycle of world trade, yet the freedom and equality of their rural property institutions is unmatched by any area of comparable size. Faced with these contradictions, the issue of living standards takes on an intractable air. Perhaps the influence of commoditisation on the standard of living is more clear-cut in industrial societies like Britain. But even here the complexity of the balance between commodity production and self-provisioning ensures that we will encounter similar analytical problems.

COMMODITISATION IN INDUSTRIAL BRITAIN

The dialectic of commodity and non-commodity production is a continuing feature of industrialisation in economies like that of Britain. Most forms of economic analysis, however, construct models

---

[33] The background to these conclusions may be found in Hart (1982a).

which ignore this central dualism. The result is that simple ideas are reified as the empirical economy. This superficial habit of mind is reinforced in the popular imagination by the preoccupation of the media with exchange rates, unemployment figures and the index of share prices. Such oversimplification is a particular obstacle to the comprehension of living standards. I would go further: no model of economic development is adequate if it fails to address explicitly the expansion of commodity economy into a world which remains constituted partly according to other principles.[34] We have become enchanted with the analytical identities of economic science or with words standing for totalities like 'capitalism' and 'socialism'. It is easy to forget that ordinary economic experience consists of a shifting combination of commodities, domestic provisioning and public organisation. The rise of public organisation in the Western economies since the First World War is not part of this paper, but the commoditisation of domestic life is.

The textile-producing populations of nineteenth-century Lancashire have exercised a powerful influence over our image of the industrial working class, not least because of the witness offered by Marx and Engels. In the following brief sketch, I draw on my knowledge of the Rossendale Valley, a cluster of towns in north-east Lancashire.[35] There is a period of about 150 years (roughly from the end of the Napoleonic wars to the present) when Rossendale's economy was dominated by coal-powered textile mills. Before then it was a fairly diversified mixture of pastoralism, transport, water-powered manufactures and local markets. Today, in an era of deindustrialisation, it is reverting to something like the pre-industrial pattern. Even at the peak of the Industrial Revolution, Rossendale's economy had a rather more plural manufacturing base than those of its neighbours. In particular, as we ought to be able to deduce from principle, it appears that this segment of the industrial proletariat was never reduced to an absolute dependence on wages, but rather

[34] See Hart (1982b). Recognition of the problem is a major strength of the Polanyi school, for example Polanyi (1944) and Bohannan and Dalton (1962). Within the Marxist tradition, Luxemburg (1951) was heavily criticised for rejecting the self-sufficiency of an analytical model of the capitalist mode of production.

[35] I have worked intermittently for some time on the economic history and ethnography of Rossendale, so far with no published result. Tupling (1927) is the basic text on the Industrial Revolution there. Lancashire figures prominently in Thompson's classic study (1968) of the world's first industrial proletariat. Manchester was Engels' (1969) home. Foster's interesting case study (1974) is partly about a Lancashire town, Oldham.

retained control over a self-generated sector of the economy which went a long way to limiting the damaging effects of downswings in factory employment. The domestic division of labour has always been anomalous, with women at times outnumbering men 2:1 as wage employees; and informal neighbourhood co-operation is very strong in communities which have experienced no significant immigration for five generations. Beyond this, the Rossendale economy included substantial amounts of small-scale strip-mining and quarrying, livestock (mainly sheep, but also poultry), transport and catering services, marketing, and the illegal recycling of goods siphoned off from the factory system. The pervasive influence of nature, with the West Pennine hills dominating the grimy towns in their folds, was reflected in a men's culture of dogs (for racing and hunting) that evokes an earlier period when the area was a royal forest. The form of industrial capitalism was highly particularistic: patriarchal mill-owners reinforced narrowly local communal identities. It would be hard to find here an abstract confrontation between the two great classes – the bourgeoisie versus a proletariat devoid of material, social and cultural resources.

The general point is that the consumption of working families was never reducible to the value of wages. An extreme example is provided by the Lancashire Cotton Famine of 1861–4, when the American Civil War sharply reduced supplies of the area's dried raw material.[36] Many mills were brought to a standstill and, especially in towns more specialised than Rossendale, the misery of the ensuing unemployment reached catastrophic proportions. Yet the damage was less than one would suppose if the working class had had no economic resources to fall back on. The fact that during this crisis Lancashire workers made persistent political representations on behalf of the North and emancipation, while the mill-owners were lobbying Parliament to help the South break the blockade of its ports, speaks of an independence of spirit which must surely have had a material foundation outside the confines of the dominant economy. Examples of the informal economy in Britain up to the present day could be multiplied.[37] But repetition of a simple point would be redundant.

---

[36] The classic study of the Lancashire cotton famine is Henderson (1969).
[37] I have written about the informal economy in a West African context (Hart 1973). Modern sociologists of Britain appear to be preoccupied with the 'hidden', 'black', 'underground' and 'informal' character of much of economic life. See, for example, Henry (1978).

The living standard under industrial capitalism is only partly a function of wages. Working people have built up their own economic resources in mitigation of erratic swings in wage employment, as well as in response to levels of wage remuneration that are often inadequate. They have also sponsored political movements which have shifted the burden of security onto a public scale of provision, making the presence and absence of the industrial welfare state perhaps the greatest contrast between living conditions in the West and in regions like the West African savanna. It will never do, therefore, to translate the economic theory of capitalism into an empirical index of the standard of living. This means that the problems of analysis and measurement we encountered first in the section on West Africa resurface in the heartland of industrial capitalism. How can the value of a partly commoditised structure of production and consumption be conceptualised, never mind quantified?

Commoditisation in the West was not finished with the outburst of factories in the nineteenth century. Further waves of technological advance (and attendant redundancy) have altered the balance between wage employment and the domestic sphere, not always in the same direction. A second industrial revolution in the decades leading up to the First World War initiated a movement to exclude women from the wage labour force.[38] At this time the parties of organised labour (including Europe's largest, the German Social Democratic Party) encouraged the seclusion of women in the home as of right, believing that middle-class families should not be alone in enjoying the privilege of a full-time domestic provider. New, highly capitalised industries (in steel, shipbuilding, chemicals, etc.) were dominated by male unions who saw high wages related to labour productivity as a chance to support their families in a novel way. Gender was always a source of stratification in labour markets (as it still is), but these developments, aimed at reducing direct competition between women and men, institutionalised a particularly extreme version of the division and offered both sides some measure of justification in neo-traditional complementarity. In this way the distinction between breadwinner and housewife was diffused through the Western working class from the 1880s onwards.

This role complex was the unchallenged form of the sexual division

---

[38] Tilly and Scott (1978).

of labour in Britain until the 1950s at least. Just as rich peasants had for centuries pulled their wives off the fields as a status symbol for their modicum of affluence, lower-middle and upper-working-class men claimed to find it unthinkable that their women should be seen to be working in public. The middle class proper, having lost their domestic servants to higher-paid wage employment, made the model seem even more general. Only the highest and lowest ranks in society were excluded from the trend, which was after all predicated on the notion that higher productivity in the wages sector should be realised as greater leisure – in the form of reduced hours for more pay, and as freedom from industrial routine for housewives. Over the last two decades or more this new social order has been rapidly dismantled – in public ideologies, if not yet in fact.[39] The main tendency of the feminist movement in this regard has been to encourage the re-entry of women into wage employment and to attack the inequalities of a stratified labour market (equal pay). This means downgrading the housewife role and insisting on the opportunity to be exploited as wage employees in ways that our grandmothers allowed their menfolk to monopolise. A subsidiary tactic has been to claim wages for housework.[40] Not the least interesting aspect of this phenomenon is the demand for wages in return for not producing commodities, reflecting both the predominance of commodity production in social life and the assumption that such a wage would be a deduction from the public purse. As industrial employment dwindles further, the institutional contrast between payment by wages (worthy citizens) and by state handout (worthless citizens) will no doubt come under increasing ideological pressure. But the point to be emphasised in this context is that 'wages for housework' draws attention to the problem of estimating the money value of domestic labour.

It is possible to break down the many components of a housewife's daily routine into services that may be purchased in the market from specialists – chauffeur, educator, nurse and so on[41] – and then to cost

---

[39] Note the synchrony of this development and of the era of the post-colonial state in West Africa, discussed in the previous section.

[40] A group of London activists currently campaign under the slogan 'wages for housework'; there is much casual literature on the topic. See Oakley (1974) for a general treatment of housework.

[41] An advertisement on British television shows a housewife and mother in a fast sequence of specialised roles, wearing the appropriate uniform of each – psychotherapist, cook, clown, first-aid nurse, even frogman (for retrieving lost objects).

them at current prices. The result is predictable: the commodity-based value of what she does is astronomically high, $70–80,000 per annum in one United States example. If the same exercise were performed for the West African savanna, the region's economic backwardness would disappear overnight. But, as we saw, market prices are themselves the outcome of the interaction between commodity production and self-provisioning. Thus, when few can afford to buy specialised services, their price is high; and because it is high most people have to do what they can for themselves. But when commodity prices fall in real terms, owing to cheaper costs of production and expanding markets, more people can afford to buy what they once regarded as a luxury for the rich. Eating out was a rare event for most people not long ago. Now that fast food is relatively cheap, fewer housewives spend every day in the kitchen. This in turn makes working for wages more feasible; and more wages means the family can afford to eat out more often. Of course, when women do work outside the home, their wages are much lower than the notional value of their housework, in part because women's pay reflects the size of the reserve army in unpaid work and the assumption of plural household incomes. Moreover, the interlocking routines of the sexual division of labour are not easily dismantled, so that many domestic duties must still be done in less time outside wage work, and some, such as pre-school childcare, represent intransigent bottlenecks for many women.

Nevertheless there is a substantial trend towards the commoditisation of domestic work in industrial societies. It has already been noted that higher labour costs have virtually eliminated domestic service of the old sort from the British economy. The re-entry of women into wage labour markets should be seen in the context of this long-run trend for labour to command higher real wages and for the cost of commodities to be cheapened. These are both aspects of a global rise in social productivity which underpins the prosperous living standards of the industrial countries. Improvements in the efficiency of labour raise the income levels of wage earners and cheapen the cost of substituting unpaid work with commodities. The aggregate level of demand for wage labour may actually fall under these circumstances, but the opportunity cost of choosing to stay at home generally rises. This means that women who prefer to look after their own children and cook their own meals now have to place a heightened moral value on these activities. It is no longer enough to justify such a life by referring to the customary division of labour alone. The emergence of a third wave of industrial expansion since the Second World War, marked by unprecedented affluence and productivity, has altered the attitude of most Western men and women to work in and out of the home. It is the evolution of commodity economy which explains why at this time the domestic seclusion of women has fallen into disrepute. These considerations never applied to the rich or the poor; but the large and flexible middle stratum of British society is deeply implicated in this tidal shift eroding the barriers that insulate the family from the world of commodities.

It is hard enough to reach agreement on the facts of this most recent instance of commoditisation. Evaluation of its effects is, if anything, even more polarised than explanations for the plight of the Third World's poor are. British children seem to think they are made better off by all these visits to fast-food restaurants. Many middle-class parents find such barbarism anathema. The death struggle of capitalism and socialism is perhaps epitomised in the hamburger. For the majority of working people, however, living standards are enhanced by the replacement of some domestic activities with commodities, in that greater flexibility is introduced into their 'functionings and capabilities'. Perhaps the value of housework is not commensurable with its market equivalents. But we do know that the two spheres directly influence each other and that, in the history of industrialisation so far, radically different notions of family life have been fostered by the advance of commodity economy. It would be as well to understand how our preconceptions have been shaped by these great swings in Western culture before reducing the level of our enquiry to the scientific measurement of living standards.

CONCLUSIONS

1. Commoditisation is a feature of both Britain and the West African savanna in modern times. The main difference is that in one case it has been accompanied by industrialisation and in the other it has not. In consequence the character of the dominant economic structure is divergent and markets play a contrasting role in social life. It appears that the institutional responses of ordinary working people in the two areas are quite similar, with domestic self-provisioning occupying in each a prominent position as a basis for long-run security. What is

grossly discrepant is the standard of living in West Africa and Britain; and that is because of the former's failure so far to embark on a trajectory in which rising labour efficiency leads to higher real wages.

2. The process of commoditisation is everywhere uneven, with marked shifts in emphasis between commodity production and self-provisioning being quite normal. Although world markets and the division of labour have advanced considerably, especially since 1945, economic downswings are intrinsic to the experience. These affect industrial and pre-industrial societies with a severity that is sometimes equal, as we have seen in the cases of the West African savanna and nineteenth-century Lancashire. It is at times of depression that the capacity of a population to draw on its resources of non-commodity production is most crucial.

3. It follows that, for most people, structures of self-provisioning are as important as markets for their livelihood. I have argued that, in view of fluctuating relations between the two, it is circular and misleading to evaluate the contribution of the non-commodity sphere to living standards by having recourse to current market prices. Under pre-industrial conditions it is quite likely that forces arising in domestic and communal organisation will shape the functioning of markets, whereas the opposite may be more true of economies driven by industrialisation.[42]

4. The status of 'the standard of living' as an object of scholarly enquiry is itself problematic. In its most abstract form, the debate is about the welfare effects of industrial capitalism, or, as I have relabelled the process, commoditisation. Clearly, social scientists confronting the poverty of the Third World are divided as to whether they think these societies need more of the Western economic formula ('the bourgeois package' of capital, cities, markets, science and the rest) or less. If our arguments are to amount to more than secular theology or propaganda for our own half-understood prejudices, they must be anchored in concrete historical enquiries. Hypothetical philosophers' examples will not do, any more than economists' indifference curves will do.

5. By placing so much emphasis on the centrality of commodities to

---

[42] This formula appears to come close to the position adopted by Polanyi's followers in substantivist economic anthropology. See notes 9 and 34 above. It differs from theirs by postulating a universal relationship between markets and subsistence organisation rather than characterising industrial and pre-industrial economies exclusively by one type of organisation or the other.

the standard of living, my approach is more sympathetic to main-stream economic analysis than Sen's appears to be. Like him I reject the utilitarian approach of the marginalists, but I draw more inspiration from the commodity-based theories of classical political economy. In particular I hold that underlying trends in labour productivity are the key to improvements in the standard of living; and these have historically depended on advances in the commercial division of labour (while being in no way guaranteed by market expansion as such). Measures of the efficiency of time allocation offer some hope for objective quantification in this field.

6. It is conceivable that the orthodox economic approach to living standards as GNP per capita bears some relation to welfare trends in a commoditised industrial economy when it is prospering. It is less relevant to ordinary living conditions in a weakly commoditised society or in any economy undergoing recession. Yet it is precisely under these latter circumstances that the standard of living becomes more of an issue. Economists rarely address the question of the relevance of their commodity- or utility-based approach to variable institutional conditions.[43] For this reason a comparative anthropological analysis of these problems may ultimately offer more penetrating insights.

---

[43] The principal exception in modern times is the American school of institutionalist economists. Galbraith's writings (e.g., 1974) are broadly within this tradition.

BERNARD WILLIAMS

The Standard of Living: Interests and Capabilities

I agree with a great deal of what Amartya Sen has said, particularly on the methodological principle which he has summed up by saying that it is better to be vaguely right than to be precisely wrong. I am also attracted to his major substantive conclusion – that we should think about these issues in terms of notions such as capabilities. I have some problems about what capabilities are. Some of them are problems particularly for Sen's formulations, while some of them are problems for all of us.

The first thing I want to refer to is a problem about what is meant by the expression 'the standard of living'. I do not want to spend very long on this; it is in some part a verbal issue, but as I think Sen brings out in his lectures, there is also at least one matter of substance here. As Sen says, 'the standard of living' is not a term of art. It is an expression that has an antecedent use, and analysis has to be responsive to that antecedent use. But I think we have to be rather cautious in testing intuitions about what really matters in this field against the established use of this particular phrase, because it may be that this particular phrase is attached to considerations, or affected by considerations, that Sen and the rest of us might well not think central. In particular, this phrase may be associated with considerations of opulence – and there may be an historical and social reason why this should be so – so that in the period in which this phrase has grown to popularity, it has been thought that well-being was particularly connected with opulence. So it might be that for historical reasons this phrase does carry some luggage which, on more general methodological grounds, we should like to take off it. Moreover, it may be unclear how far it is affected in this way, so we do not even have a totally clear programme for removing these associations.

I think it is worth distinguishing three different things that one may be talking about in these connections. In his second lecture Sen refers to a distinction between what Pigou called 'economic welfare' and 'total welfare', and he mentioned the fact (which I think, if I follow him, Pigou also mentioned) that the idea of total welfare could include the satisfaction of altruistic desires, whereas economic welfare would not be taken to include the satisfaction of altruistic desires. There is another distinction, and this is very closely related to what Sen mentions in his second lecture as 'Aśoka's distinction'. Aśoka noted the fact that I may be afflicted by an injury to another person, even though I am myself 'well provided for'. This, too, is thought to shed some light on the distinction between the standard of living notion and the general well-being notion.

We therefore have several phrases in play here: 'total welfare', 'economic welfare', 'standard of living', and 'well-being'. It does not matter much what we do with these four phrases, as long as we get some clarity about what we are doing with them, which is what Sen is seeking to do. I should like to suggest that we need to distinguish three ideas. The first idea is that of everything that an agent has reason to favour or promote – everything that for whatever reasons he or she is in favour of, or would like to happen, either to him- or herself, or to society or anywhere. The second notion is the same as the first one, minus all the desires or objectives that do not refer to the agent him- or herself; we leave out desires for states of affairs that do not either directly or indirectly involve the agent's own satisfaction. This yields a narrower notion of, roughly, ego-centred items, that is things people have reason to promote for a reason that is connected with themselves. That is a very vague notion and there are many problems with it, but I take it to be something like the notion of a person's interests. This is a narrower notion than the first. Somebody may have very good reason to promote other people's welfare, for altruistic or other reasons, but we naturally say that he or she is acting in somebody else's interests, not in his or her own interests. As well as speaking of the agent's own interests, I shall sometimes use the term 'well-being' for this idea. The third and narrowest notion is the notion of an agent's economic interests, and I think that it is to this notion that the phrase 'the standard of living' is attached. I do not really know what the class of somebody's economic interests are and, because of that, I shall not spend any time on this notion.

It seems to me that for a lot of the time in his lectures Sen is discussing the second of these notions, that of somebody's interests or well-being, rather than some narrower class of his economic interests. However, we have to bear in mind here a question which Sen properly reminds us of more than once, namely what the practical relevance of the idea of the standard of living is, what the motivation is for using this notion. We need to put into the argument the connection between the concept of the standard of living and the concept of government action, or other forms of public action. One thing we may have in mind, when we talk about the standard of living, as a notion narrower than that of a whole set of people's individual interests, is the matter of which interests can be effectively and legitimately affected, in a direct way, by government policy. What kinds of interest should it be the aim of government policy in various ways to promote, and how may it affect them? Reflection on those questions might, indeed, help us to see why a particular subclass of people's interests – roughly, their economic interests – should be naturally picked out by the phrase 'the standard of living'.

I now turn to the question of identifying capabilities. If we say – and it is clearly a sympathetic suggestion – that an agent's interests are particularly connected with the capabilities that the agent may possess or lack, we need some idea of what counts as a capability.

Sen raises the question of how capability is related to functioning, and he directs our attention to the idea that capability stands to functioning as the possible stands to the actual. However, things are more complicated than this may make them seem. There is certainly a valid inference from 'is' to 'can'. As the scholastic maxim put it, *ab esse ad posse valet consequentia* – the fact that something is actual tells one that it is possible. So if someone is actually doing something, then it follows that he can do it, in the modest sense that it is possible that he should do it. But it does not follow from this that in a sense relevant to these discussions he has a capability or capacity to do it.

Suppose we pass through a room and hear and see a man singing. He is actually singing, and so, by the maxim, he can sing. But then we learn that he is deranged, and sings all the time – indeed, sings just like that all the time. Then his singing is not an expression of the capability that we normally associate with singing, which involves, among other things, the capability of not singing. The point applies to the term 'functioning'. If actually singing is enough to establish 'functioning' in that respect, then, of course, the madman's singing is an example of it; on that assumption, we should not say that functioning necessarily implies a substantive or relevant capability. But it is more natural, in fact, to uphold the connection between functioning and capability, and say rather that the madman's singing is not an example, in the relevant sense, of functioning. In order to establish that given pieces of behaviour are examples of a certain kind of functioning we may, rather, have to establish that they are expressions of the relevant capability.

There are several important questions about the ways in which capability is related to possibility, and also to the notion of an ability. I should like to ask four questions about capabilities, as Sen uses that notion in his argument. I shall try to give answers to one or two of them, but I am not sure how to systematise the answers, while in other cases I do not know what the answer should be.

The first question is: if someone possesses a capability, must that person have the capacity or opportunity to choose? The answer seems to be that in some cases, at least, he or she must have that opportunity if the surrounding possibilities are to count as a capability at all. Suppose I live in the Republic of Authoritania. In Authoritania, we all get a holiday paid for by the state, but we get posted to a particular resort. Every year I am posted to the desirable holiday resort of Chernenkograd. Have I the capability to go to Chernenkograd? Well, I go there, and so, by the maxim, I can; if capability were just a matter of possibility, then I would have the capability. But no one would call this, in the relevant sense, a capability. It might be said that it is a capability, but not the one we are relevantly interested in: it is the capability to go to Chernenkograd, but that is all it is, and that is not enough. Suppose, then, that the regime becomes a little more liberal, and now I do not always go to Chernenkograd – some years I get posted there and other years I get posted somewhere else. Have I now the capability to go to the one place or the other? Surely not, in any sense of 'capability' relevantly related to well-being. In this sort of case, I surely must have the opportunity to choose. This immediately raises the question as to whether I have more capabilities, the more choices I have available to me, that is a question I shall come back to shortly.

The first question, then, is: Do capabilities entail the opportunity or ability to choose? The answer seems to be that at least some of them do. The second question is: Do *all* capabilities entail the opportunity or ability to choose? The answer to that may well be 'no', as Sen is using the idea, since he cites as an example in his second lecture, when comparing the standard of living in India and in China, the fact that life expectation is higher in China than it is in India. He interprets the relevance of life expectation to the standard of living in terms of capabilities. But what capability is it that is increased by an increase in the expectation of life? It is hard to see how an increase in choice can be involved, at least choice in respect of life and death: it would be very odd to suppose that an increase in life expectation contributes to my well-being or standard of living because it gives me a longer time in which to choose whether to commit suicide. (Suppose the society were strongly conditioned against even considering suicide. Would you increase their standard of living or well-being by removing that conditioning, so that people were more disposed to choose?) It does not look as though everything that Sen counts as a capability is directly related, at least, to choice. A capability certainly need not be related to choice over the good that itself contributes to the increase in well-being or the standard of living, though choice may, of course, be introduced in some other, less direct, way.

The third question is: How do we count capabilities? There is a danger of trivialisation here, in particular if one simply generates capabilities from commodities. It may be said that every time we multiply commodities, we multiply capabilities. If we create a new washing powder, 'Bloppo', then we shall have thereby created a new capability, the capability of choosing 'Bloppo'. Indeed, advertisers are always telling us that our freedom or our capabilities are being extended because there is yet another form of washing powder that previously we could not choose because it did not exist, but which now we can choose.

On that line of argument, any increase in the commodities available must create some new capabilities, simply by logical necessity. Equally by logical necessity, of course, it will be true that the creation of a new commodity also takes away capabilities. If I introduce 'Bloppo', again, it takes away the capability (perhaps slightly more substantial) of only having to choose between three washing powders; and so on. All this is obviously a trivial multiplication of capabilities, and it is not going to count. But how do we decide what does count as a significant extension of capabilities?

My fourth and last question about capabilities is: How is the capability of doing X related to the actual ability to do X now? Earlier questions concerned the relation between capability and possibility; this is a similar sort of question, concerning the relation between capability and ability. Presumably we want to say that in some sense, if agents possess the capability to do X, then they must possess the ability to do X – it must be true of them that they can do X. But what does 'can do X' in these circumstances mean? In another paper on this subject (1984b), very closely related in content to his lectures, Sen gives an example of a capability strongly relevant to the standard of living, the capability of breathing unpolluted air. This was introduced precisely to make the point that one should not think of the standard of living in terms simply of basic needs, or simply in terms of commodities or services, but should think of it in terms of capabilities. What you are giving people, or taking away from them, in relation to pollution, is the capability of breathing unpolluted air, which is assumed to be a desirable capability. But consider the inhabitant of Los Angeles who, it is said, cannot breathe unpolluted air. It is not true that he cannot breathe unpolluted air. He can do so, but he has to go somewhere else to do it. Admittedly, he cannot do it here and now, but *he can do it* does not entail *he can do it here and now*. Indeed, if we are to make the notion of capability central to ideas of well-being or the standard of living, we must not insist that a capability necessarily involves the ability to do the relevant thing here and now.

This is connected to a point that Sen himself mentions when discussing functioning. If I have a choice between doing A and doing B, and I choose to do A, it will probably no longer be the case that I can do B – I shall no longer be in a position to do it. But that does not mean I have lost a capability. The capability is of a higher order, and a number of conditions may have to be fulfilled, granted my present situation, before a capability that I have will express itself in action. But this raises very substantial problems. How far should we consider the costs of doing something, when we are trying to decide whether someone has the capability of doing it? For instance, is it the case that I can go to Cortina d'Ampezzo for the winter? Well, I *could* go to that resort for the winter: it would merely involve my deserting my family, resigning my job, mortgaging my house, and going even further and irremediably into overdraft. So I can go, but there is a very high cost attached to it. Is it a capability that I have? This is the same question as that about the man in Los Angeles, who can breathe fresh air, but has to go somewhere else to do it, something that of course involves costs.

All this yields, I think, two points, both of which suggest that the arguments about capability need to be taken further. One is that it is very doubtful that you can take capabilities singly in thinking about these questions: you have to think about sets of co-realisable capabilities, and about social states in which people acquire various ranges of capability. This is connected both with the 'Bloppo' problem, the fabrication of capabilities by trivial means, and also with the point I raised last, about the costs involved in realising a certain potentiality or ability – the cost is often a cost in terms of the capacity to do something else, as in the example about the winter resort.

Sen may well, if I understand his position, not mind accepting this first point, as perhaps a complication of the thesis, but one in the same spirit. The second point may be more difficult for his view. This is the suggestion, which certainly some people wish to advance, that these problems cannot be solved by reference to capabilities in themselves, but that you have to introduce the notion of a right. The apparently innocent and descriptive-looking notions of the standard of living or well-being may then turn out to contain considerations about those goods to which we believe people have a basic right. Thus we actually believe that people have a basic right to breathe clean air without having to go somewhere else to do it, but we do not believe that they have a similar right to go to expensive winter holiday resorts. I am not very happy myself with taking rights as the starting point. The notion of a basic human right seems to me obscure enough, and I would rather come at it from the perspective of basic human capabilities. I would prefer capabilities to do the work, and if we are going to have a language or rhetoric of rights, to have it delivered from them, rather than the other way round. But I think that there remains an unsolved problem: how we should see the relations between these concepts.

The questions that I have raised about capabilities and their identification all suggest that one has to put some constraints on the kinds of capability that are going to count in thinking about the relation between capability on the one hand and well-being or the standard of living on the other. In fact, I have slipped into that, by starting to talk about *basic* capabilities, and I think that it is difficult to avoid taking into account the notion of something like a basic capability, or (if the suggestion is adopted that I mentioned earlier) a basic set of capabilities.

Where are these constraints to come from? Traditionally they have come either from nature or from convention, or, perhaps, from some more sophisticated combination of the two. Sen brings in Adam Smith's admirable example of the man in the linen shirt, the man who cannot appear, given his society's arrangements and expectations, without shame in public unless he has a linen shirt; and Sen makes the point that here a variance in the space of commodities may mirror an invariance in the space of capabilities. What you need, in order to appear without shame in public, differs depending on where you are, but there is an invariant capability here, namely that of appearing in public without shame. This underlying capability is more basic. We do not rest with the capability to appear in a shirt, to appear in a linen shirt, to appear in a linen shirt washed with 'Bloppo', but rather invoke an underlying capability to appear without shame in public; and that, in its turn, might be derived from some yet more basic capability, such as the capability to command the materials of self-respect. At this point, the capability theory joins up, in this particular respect, with Rawls' (1971) theory, which includes the materials of self-respect among primary goods. Indeed, Sen has suggested, in discussing Rawls' views, that primary goods are best understood in terms of capabilities.

In what sense is the capability to appear without shame in public (or some yet more general capability) basic or fundamental? The suggestion might be that it is derived from some universal and fundamental fact about human beings. But what kind of fact will this be: that people want to appear in public without shame, that they need to, that shame is a universal human reaction, or what? This is a question of how we represent the universal human facts. Are they themselves to be represented in terms of capabilities, or rather in terms of needs or drives or wants or frustrations? Do we come out of the terminology of capabilities again, when we turn to their natural basis?

In any case, there is a question of the extent to which the capabilities relevant to determine problems about well-being or the standard of living all have a natural basis. I suspect that the story is bound to be mixed between nature and convention. We may be able, up to a point, to draw considerations from theories of human nature, but beyond that point we shall need to appeal to local cultural significances. We shall want to say that certain capabilities are important in a given society because in that society the cultural understandings legitimate or emphasise certain possibilities. (It is instructive to compare the impossibilities of finding, respectively, a German-speaking postal official in Taunton, a French-speaking postal official in Medicine Hat, Alberta, and a French-speaking postal official in some township in French Canada.) But we shall also have to bear in mind that we cannot simply take without correction the locally recognised capacities and incapacities, opportunities and lack of opportunities, because in some cases the question of what is recognised will be ideological in just the respects that are under discussion. The incapacity to find a Buddhist Temple in Taunton or Medicine Hat may be uncontentious, but what about the incapacity to find a Roman Catholic church in an Islamic state? Someone may say that there, equally, there is no frustration, since there are no Roman Catholics around. But what about the incapacity in some Islamic state to find a girls' school that goes beyond the elementary level? Again it will be said that no one is frustrated by this, because the girls do not want to go to school. Perhaps they do not want to go to school, beyond some elementary and socially approved level, but critics think that this itself is produced by the low level of well-being, in this respect, that obtains in such a state.

We have to correct the local expectations of what count as relevant opportunities and lack of opportunities in the light of general social theory and general ethical criticism of these societies. We may well have to do that in terms of some doctrine or other of real interests; traditionally at least, such criticisms have used a doctrine of real interests, which of course in turn may or may not cycle back to theories of human nature and the grounding of the enterprise in terms of what we count as basic capacities, interests and so on.

My conclusion, then, is that the notion of capabilities is in fact a very important contribution to thinking about these basic questions of human interests, and this leads us quite a long way from the narrower notion of economic interests, or, again, of the standard of living in its more conventional acceptation. I agree entirely with Sen about this. However, there are many pressing questions about the identification of what a capability is, and they cannot be answered without a good deal of further theory. We are forced to ask what kinds of facts are presented by human nature in these respects, and also how we should interpret local convention. Those questions are likely to turn back to some traditional but still very pressing problems about such things as real interests.

AMARTYA SEN

Reply

I am extremely grateful to the four distinguished commentators for their marvellously engaging and stimulating (as well as kind) remarks on my Tanner Lectures. They have raised a number of interesting and important issues, and in my reply I shall concentrate on only a few of them. I have chosen those points on which I may possibly have something to add to what has already been said by the commentators themselves.

I agree with most of the points made by John Muellbauer in his constructive and far-reaching rejoinder, especially his exploration of the influence of habits and psychology on living standards as well as his pointer to the fact that some approaches to 'equivalence scales' (especially that due to Rothbarth) reveal more about inequality within the household than other approaches do. I also agree that one can get help from the literature on index numbers and inequality measurement in exploring a metric for freedom. However, as he himself notes, there are problems with each of these approaches, and it is really hard to think of some method of precipitating a complete ordering of freedom (seen as a complete ordering of *sets* of achievable alternatives) on the basis of a complete ordering of particular achievements. One can certainly extend the 'dominance partial ordering', but there is a trade-off between completeness on the one hand and relevance on the other. I have tried to discuss this question in my *Commodities and Capabilities*,[1] in which I have also tried to explore several other methods of extending the dominance partial ordering.

Muellbauer is also right in drawing attention to the analogy

---

[1] Sen (1985a: Chapter 7). See also the technical literature cited there on the ranking of sets on the basis of the ranking of elements.

between 'functionings' and the 'fundamental commodities' produced by households, as outlined in the approach of 'household production function' developed by Gary Becker (1976, 1981) and others. He is right to point out that the 'rather restrictive assumptions' with which the household production view is associated (to derive results about 'implicit markets, extending the economics of the market place to the household') are not intrinsic to the approach. I accept that analogy, and I would certainly have no difficulty in agreeing that there is a similarity between 'functionings' and these 'fundamental commodities'. But it is also arguable that this analogy can be misleading since functionings are features of the state of existence of a person and they cannot be easily seen as detached objects that the person or the household happen to 'own' or 'produce'. Being free from disease, or living long, or not being 'ashamed to appear in public' (a consideration analysed by Adam Smith in the *Wealth of Nations*) can be seen as commodities only in a very peculiar sense, and it is worth asking whether this analogy – and it is no more than an analogy – is a particularly useful one for economic analysis, whether formal or informal. The questions that are suggested by the analogy may not often be particularly appropriate, for example what is 'the time required to produce a unit of that commodity' (Becker 1976:6).[2] Furthermore, many of the functionings (e.g., living a life free from cholera or smallpox) are 'produced' at least as much *outside* the household as *inside* it (e.g., through public policy against epidemics). I would, therefore, argue that the analogy with the 'household production function' is restricted not only by the rather severe assumptions that Becker and others make to develop the results regarding 'implicit markets' (see Muellbauer 1974b and Pollak and Wachter 1975), but also by the very conception of 'commodities' in the household production approach, which differs substantially from 'functionings' as explored in my lectures (and in Sen 1982, 1985a).

Muellbauer's pointer to the analogy with 'human development' indicators is also illuminating, and indeed less problematic. However, these indicators can be of any kind whatsoever, and the diverse literature brings out the variety of indicators that have been thought of. The concentration on 'functionings' and 'capabilities' represents the selection of a particular class of relevant indicators, and in this respect the approach examined here, in the context of the standard of

---

[2] On this question, see Sen (1985a: 15–16).

living, must be seen as more discriminating. There is, in fact, a need to assess the motivation underlying the use of any set of indicators, and it can be argued that the approach of development indicators (as well as that of 'basic needs') would have to stand up to the challenge of more classical approaches based on 'utility' and other foundational concepts. As I have tried to discuss in my second lecture, even utilitarian economists like Pigou could strongly argue in favour of an approach that is essentially that of 'basic needs' but *founded on utilitarian principles*. The basic needs approach is, in this sense, not necessarily a rival to the utilitarian view, for the issue of rivalry comes up only in the context of examining the *foundations* of the concentration on 'basic needs'. It is in this context that the arguments for the intrinsic relevance of functionings and freedom become particularly important.

These are some differences of emphasis, but in general I feel very much in sympathy with the extensions, developments and interpretations presented in Muellbauer's extremely helpful and creative rejoinder.

Ravi Kanbur has thrown light on a particular aspect of the accounting of living standards in particular and individual advantage in general. This concerns uncertainties, and Kanbur has brought out clearly and illuminatingly how the *ex post* view differs systematically from the *ex ante* view. He comes out in favour of the *ex post* magnitudes for judging advantage, and I see the force of his reasoning in the examples he considers. (I only wish he would not refer to what 'Sen would argue' in his hypothetical example of 'Sen' receiving some advantage and trying to defend it – lousily in my judgement – against the claims of *ex post* equality!)

There is an important difference between a 'capability set' from which the person chooses an element (the choice is one's own) and the 'possible outcome set' in 'uncertainty analysis' (the choice is *not* one's own). *Ex ante* advantages in the context of the latter are indeed discountable for reasons presented by Kanbur. These reasons, however, would do little to discount the *ex ante* advantage of the former kind (when the choice is one's own and when the outcome reflects one's choice). My discussion on capability and advantage related to that former case, in contrast with Kanbur's concentration on the latter. I state this for the sake of clarification only, and I do not expect Kanbur to disagree on the different relevance of the two types of *ex ante* sets.

If I have any disagreement with Ravi Kanbur, it concerns his treatment of the limitation of 'dominance reasoning' in ranking capabilities in general and living standards in particular. He is certainly right that the introduction of uncertainty makes the dominance reasoning more limited. This is particularly so when we are trying to arrive at an overall evaluation of a social state involving different individuals, and that seems to be the problem with which he is immediately concerned. However, in the context of judging the living standard of a particular individual, dominance reasoning may or may not be quite so limited. For example, in his hypothetical illustration, Kanbur ends with recommending 'taking some cake away from Sen and giving it to Williams', and points out that he 'would not be much persuaded by arguments that such an arrangement would in fact lead to a catastrophic reduction in the standard of living of both'.

This is certainly right, but there is no question that taking the cake away from 'Sen' would reduce *his* standard of living (whether or not catastrophically is a different issue altogether). The hypothetical Sen's freedom to enter the lottery would have been compromised and, furthermore, he would have less of the cake. Other things given, this is certainly a reduction of the living standard of the hypothetical Sen. In the case of the hypothetical Williams, there *is* a conflict. He has less freedom to participate in lotteries but has more cake in the outcome. However, the existence of this conflict should not make us overlook the absence of ambiguity in dominance reasoning in the calculation of the hypothetical Sen's living standard, and that reasoning may well work clearly enough in judging personal living standards. The public policy question of what should be done in this case cannot, of course, be determined by 'dominance' since that involves 'Williams' as well as 'Sen', and the scope of dominance reasoning is indeed very much more limited when *social aggregation* is considered. But this was not in fact the focus of my lectures (though, in general, I have nothing against 'social choice' as a subject). Dominance reasoning takes us further in the determination of *personal* living standards than in resolving *interpersonal conflicts*.

Keith Hart's engaging paper raises a number of interesting questions and presents a useful and important analysis of the living standard, seen particularly in the perspective of the production and use of what he calls 'commodities'. I see the relevance of his argument, though perhaps I should warn that the use of the term 'commodities' in his analysis is somewhat different from that commonly used in modern economics. What he calls 'self-provisioning' (in contrast with 'commodity production') may also involve what in the jargon of modern economics is called 'commodities' (e.g., food produced for consumption within the family producing it). But once that 'nominal' point is sorted out, it is perfectly clear what Hart is saying and why.

Hart notes that his approach is 'more sympathetic to mainstream economic analysis than Sen's appears to be'. I am not sure whether that contrast is exactly clear. He emphasises that he holds 'that underlying trends in labour productivity are the key to improvements in the standard of living'. This would appear to be an assertion about the *causation* of changes in the standard of living, rather than about the way of *conceptualising* that standard. Even if the standard of living is seen in terms of 'functionings' and 'capabilities' (as I argue), it could still be plausible to argue that 'trends in labour productivity are the key to improvements in the standard of living'. The question that I addressed concerns the way the standard of living is to be seen, characterised and measured.

Trends in labour productivity affect the living standard through a rather complicated process. The increase in the overall availability of commodities as a result of an increase in labour productivity could lead to an increase in the standard of living of different sections of the population, depending on the *distribution* of the aggregate supply and the *utilisation* of commodities in giving people the ability to do this or be that. Hart's causal analysis is thus primarily concerned with a rather different question from the one that I addressed in my lectures. I must, therefore, simultaneously assert both the importance of the questions raised by Hart and the fact that some of these questions are rather different from mine.

Finally, I turn to Bernard Williams' friendly questioning of the approach that I have tried to develop. The friendliness of his style should not make us overlook the fact that he is asking very hard questions, which could possibly make a major dent in the approach presented in my lectures.

One of the things that comes out very clearly from Williams' analysis is the inescapable need for different valuation exercises for adequately pursuing the capabilities approach to the living standard. (John Dunn's remarks in the discussion also contributed to the understanding of the relevance and centrality of this issue.) Certainly, any pointer to the pre-eminence of 'functionings' and 'capabilities' in the assessment of the living standard is doing no more than specifying an appropriate 'space' in which the valuation has to be performed, rather than doing the valuation itself. I do not find it a matter of great embarrassment that some of these valuational questions may turn out to be difficult, controversial, and perhaps, in some cases, even undecidable (leading to *partial orderings* of living standards). I have tried to argue elsewhere that though 'it is valuation with which we are ultimately concerned in the functionings approach' (1985a:32), this does not reduce the importance of the 'space', that is of concentrating on 'functioning' and 'capabilities'. Nor does this do anything to rehabilitate the utility-based approaches. The utilitarian approach also involves valuation, in that case of an allegedly homogeneous magnitude (to wit, utility), and while the valuation function takes simply a monotonic and straightforward form (and can even be seen as an identity mapping), the fact that some valuation is being explicitly or implicitly made must be recognised. The inherent plurality of 'functionings' and 'capabilities' does not change the fundamental necessity of valuation, and the homogeneous singularity of utility – even if true – does not alter this basic necessity. Williams is also right to emphasise that the exercise of valuation must involve a mixture of 'nature' and 'convention'.[3]

It is also the recognition of the necessity of valuation that helps to sort out such cases as the capabilities *added* and *subtracted* as a result of the introduction of a new washing powder called 'Bloppo', discussed by Williams. The question is not so much about 'the identification of what a capability is', but more about the valuation of different capabilities. Many capabilities may be trivial and valueless, while others are substantial and important. The advantage that is achieved by concentrating on the space of functionings and capabilities does not eliminate the necessity of these valuations in the context of judging living standards of individuals, households and nations. It is not even, I believe, a matter of only putting 'some constraints on the kinds of capability that are going to count'. It calls for a more discriminating exercise of valuing different capabilities differently, varying from the extremely important to the completely trivial. The

---

[3] The relevance of convention does not, however, deny the need for critical assessment, or suggest automatic acceptance of conventional values. Some of the difficult issues in the valuational problem were discussed briefly in my second lecture; see also Sen (1985a: Chapters 3–5).

contribution of 'Bloppo' possibly does happen to lie clearly at the latter end, but there can be more complex cases.

The relevance of what Williams refers to as '*basic* capabilities' becomes particularly clear, not so much in ranking living standards, but in deciding on a cut-off point for the purpose of assessing poverty and deprivation.[4] This takes the form of a 'constraint' because we are looking for a cut-off point to determine whether people are in poverty or not. On the other hand, in doing a *ranking* of living standards, we need a more discriminating valuational approach. Williams asks the question as to whether 'the notion of a basic human right' might be helpful in the context of judging the living standard. I do not believe it can be particularly helpful in *ranking* living standards in general, but it may have great relevance in the specific context of assessing poverty and deprivation.

Turning now to Williams' suggestion that we must look at 'sets of co-realisable capabilities', I must assert complete agreement. Indeed the achievement of functionings must always be seen as n-tuples (sometimes representable as vectors, but not always), and capabilities have to be seen as *sets* of such n-tuples. In this 'multidimensional' format, there is thus no particular problem in dealing with the ability of the inhabitant of Los Angeles to breathe unpolluted air. If that person migrates in search of fresh air, that alternative must be seen in terms of the post-migration n-tuple of *all* functionings. The objects that are ranked are n-tuples of functionings and sets of such n-tuples, i.e. capabilities (Sen 1985a: Chapters 2, 6, 7).

Williams' threefold distinction between (1) 'everything that an agent has reason to favour or promote', (2) *that* 'minus all the desires or objectives that do not refer to the agent him- or herself', and (3) 'the notion of an agent's economic interests', is a very useful one. Williams argues that it is the category of 'economic interests' that 'should be naturally picked out by the phrase "the standard of living"'. There is, I think, considerable plausibility in this diagnosis. (It is in fact a position rather close to the one I actually took in Sen 1984b.) But I am not entirely persuaded by it, since the quality of life and what can be described as the standard of living one succeeds in achieving may well incorporate factors other than the purely economic. For example, if one suffers from an incurable disease, clearly that must be seen as reducing one's standard of living (in addition to affecting the

---

[4] I have tried to discuss this question in Sen (1983a).

'quantity' of one's life), and this may not depend only on economic influences. There is something to argue about here, and as I said in my lectures, I have somewhat changed my position from the Pigovian focus on the purely 'economic' to a rather broader characterisation of the standard of living. It is possible, however, that what I have done amounts to an *over*broadening of the notion. Williams suggests that my discussion of the standard of living is more concerned with 'well-being, rather than some narrower class of . . . economic interests'. While I do think the living standard is broader than economic interests, I also believe that there is a distinction between 'well-being' and 'standard of living'. The latter figures *in between* Williams' category (2) to category (3), I would argue.

Category (2) includes all reasons connected with one's own welfare. Some of these connections are direct, for example pursuing one's own nutrition, and some are indirect, for example pursuing the removal of general poverty on the grounds that it pains one to see other people in misery. In defining 'the standard of living' I was planning to eliminate the latter type of reason, which relates primarily to the lives of others, but to include the former, which relates directly to one's own life. If this intermediate category between (2) and (3) is called (2*), then (2*) is where the line is drawn, with 'the standard of living' being something in between Williams' category (2) of 'ego-centred items', and category (3) of 'economic interests'. The rationale of taking this more inclusive view than Williams' (3) of a person's living standard is to admit the influence of non-economic features that directly affect one's life (e.g., the absence of morbidity) in the notion of the standard of living, taking the living standard to be rather broader than economic interests.[5]

It is hard to be sure that one has got all this exactly right, and in any case, as Williams rightly emphasises, the usefulness of a particular definition of the standard of living depends much on what use we intend to make of it. I can see much use for Williams' categories, but I think there is a case for using the intermediate category (2*) as well,[6] as a relevant characterisation of the standard of living.

---

[5] Illness and death are of course partly influenceable by economic factors (e.g., they are affected by income and wealth). But there are *other* influences as well. But no matter what the influences are, being ill or being dead clearly does affect the quality and the standard of one's living.

[6] In contrast with category (1), Williams' category (2) includes 'sympathy' but not 'commitment', in the language used in Sen (1977a); see also Williams (1973). Category (2*) drops 'sympathy' as well. Williams' category (3) will also drop self-centred non-economic reasons.

Finally, I should make a brief remark on Williams' extremely interesting arguments suggesting that a capability to do something must imply the ability of doing the *opposite*. I see the force of the argument, but I am less sure of the precise conclusion to be drawn. We sometimes have the ability to do things in a genuine sense without being able to do the opposite. For example, Ann may have the ability not to marry Bill (no matter what Bill wants), if she so chooses, but this does not imply that she has the ability to marry Bill (i.e., *not not* marry Bill) if she chooses (irrespective of Bill's views). Similarly, Bill may be able to end his own life whenever he chooses without being able always to keep on living. Some abilities have a natural asymmetry, and it would be unreasonable to insist that a particular capability can be real only if the ability to do the opposite is also present.

Of course, what the alternatives are must be relevant to the notion of what in the lectures I have called 'refined functionings' (see also Sen 1985a, 1985b). For example, *fasting* in the sense of starving when one has the alternative of not starving is quite different from starving when one has no such alternative. In my exercises, it is relevant to consider what other opportunities exist, and this certainly is an important point in characterising functionings in a 'refined' way.[7] But in general one could question the belief that a person's capability to do $\propto$ *must* imply his or her ability to do *not* $\propto$, without fail. One might be able to do $\propto$ whenever one chooses, but one's efforts at doing *not* $\propto$ may well be sometimes successful and sometimes not. In such a situation a person does have the capability to achieve $\propto$, but *not* the full capability to achieve *not* $\propto$.

Williams points out that there remain 'many pressing questions' concerning the approach to the standard of living that I have tried to present and that 'they cannot be answered without a good deal of further theory'. I agree with this completely and had ended my lectures by asserting that we have 'a long way to go'. Even if the basic

[7] Williams questions my view that 'capability stands to functioning as the possible stands to the actual'. His example concerning the person who is 'deranged, and sings all the time' may, in fact, be re-examined in terms of the 'refined' functionings of 'singing' when the person has the ability *not* to produce such sounds. This would support Williams' diagnosis that 'the madman's singing is not an example, in the relevant sense, of functioning'. But if one *is* achieving a functioning in the relevant sense, then one does have the *capability* to function, in *that* sense. The characterisation of 'the capability set' as a set of *n*-tuples of functionings, *including* the *n*-tuple *actually* achieved (in the absence of uncertainty), is consistent with different interpretations of functionings, including the 'refined' (e.g., the madman is *not* really 'singing') as well as the 'unrefined' (he *is*).

move towards functionings and capabilities is accepted (as I believe it should be, for reasons that I have tried to present), there will remain many difficult and perplexing questions to answer. But as the illuminating comments of Williams, and those of Muellbauer, Kanbur and Hart, show quite clearly, it is possible to address many of these questions in a constructive way and to move forward. I could not have asked for more, and I *am* grateful.

Bibliography

Adelman, I. and Morris, C. T. 1973. *Economic Growth and Social Equity in Developing Countries*. Stanford: Stanford University Press

Akerlof, G. 1983. Loyalty filters. *American Economic Review*, 73

Allardt, S. 1981. Experiences from the comparative Scandinavian welfare study, with a bibliography of the project. *European Journal of Political Research*, 9

Arrow, K. J. 1963. *Social Choice and Individual Values*. New York: Wiley

Arrow, K. J. 1971. *Essays in the Theory of Risk Bearing*. Amsterdam: North-Holland

Ashton, B., Hill, K., Piazza, A. and Zeitz, R. 1984. Famine in China, 1958–61. *Population and Development Review*, 10

Barten, A. 1964. Family composition prices and expenditure patterns. In *Econometric Analysis for National Economic Planning*, ed. P. E. Hart, G. Mills and J. K. Whitaker. London: Butterworth

Basu, K. 1979. *Revealed Preference of the Government*. Cambridge: Cambridge University Press

Bauer, P. T. 1954. *West African Trade*. Cambridge: Cambridge University Press

Becker, G. S. 1965. A theory of the allocation of time. *Economic Journal*, 75

Becker, G. S. 1976. *The Economic Approach to Human Behaviour*. Chicago: University of Chicago Press

Becker, G. S. 1981. *A Treatise on the Family*. Cambridge MA: Harvard University Press

Beckerman, W. and Clark, S. 1982. *Poverty and Social Security in Britain since 1961*. Oxford: Clarendon Press

Bentham, J. 1970 [1789]. *An Introduction to the Principles of Morals and Legislation*, ed. J. H. Burns and H. L. A. Hart. London: Athlone Press

Blackorby, C. 1975. Degrees of cardinality and aggregate partial ordering. *Econometrica*, 43

Bohannan, P. and Dalton, G. (eds.) 1962. *Markets in Africa*. Evanston: Northwestern University Press

Broome, J. 1978. Choice and value in economics. *Oxford Economic Papers*, 30

Broome, J. 1984. Uncertainty and fairness. *Economic Journal*, 94

Cantril, H. 1965. *The Pattern of Human Concerns*. New Brunswick NJ: Rutgers University Press

Chichilnisky, G. 1980. Basic needs and global models: resources, trade and distribution. *Alternatives*, 6

Cipolla, C. 1978. *The Economic History of World Population*. Harmondsworth: Penguin

Cleave, J. 1974. *African Farmers: Labour Use in the Development of Smallholder Agriculture*. New York: Praeger

Comité d'Information Sahel 1975. *Qui se nourrit de la famine en Afrique? Le dossier politique de la faim au Sahel*. Paris: Maspero

Cooter, R. and Rappoport, P. 1984. Were the ordinalists wrong about welfare economics? *Journal of Economic Literature*, 22

Copans, J. (ed.) 1975. *Sécheresses et famines du Sahel*. Paris: Maspero

Costa, P. T. and McCrae, R. R. 1980. Influence of extroversion and neuroticism on subjective well-being: happy and unhappy people. *Journal of Personality and Social Psychology*, 38

Dalby, D. and Church, R. J. H. (eds.) 1973. *Drought in Africa*. London: School of Oriental and African Studies

Deane, P. 1969. *The First Industrial Revolution*. Cambridge: Cambridge University Press

Deaton, A. 1981. *Three Essays on a Sri Lanka Household Survey*. Living Standards Measurement Study Working Paper no. 11. Washington DC: World Bank

Deaton, A. and Muellbauer, J. 1980. *Economics and Consumer Behaviour*. Cambridge: Cambridge University Press

Deaton, A. and Muellbauer, J. 1986. On measuring child costs with applications to poor countries. *Journal of Political Economy*, 94

Deaton, A., Ruiz-Castillo, J. and Thomas, D. 1985. The influence of household composition on household expenditure patterns: theory and Spanish evidence. Princeton University, Research Program in Development Studies, discussion paper, 122

Diamond, P. A. 1967. Cardinal welfare, individualist ethics, and interpersonal comparisons of utility. *Journal of Political Economy*, 59

Dobb, M. 1973. *Theories of Value and Distribution since Adam Smith*. Cambridge: Cambridge University Press

Dworkin, R. 1980. Is wealth a value? *Journal of Legal Studies*, 9

Easterlin, R. A. 1974. Does economic growth improve the human lot? In *Nations and Households in Economic Growth*, ed. P. A. David and M. W. Reder. New York: Academic Press

Elster, J. 1983. *Sour Grapes*. Cambridge: Cambridge University Press

Engel, E. 1895. Die Lebenskosten belgischer Arbeiterfamilien früher und jetzt. *International Statistical Institute Bulletin*, 9

Engels, F. 1969 [1892]. *The Condition of the Working Class in England.* London: Panther

Erikson, R., Hansen, E. J., Ringen, S. and Uusitalo, H. 1984. *The Scandinavian way: the welfare states and welfare research.* Mimeo

Fiegehen, G. C., Lansley, P. S. and Smith, A. D. 1977. *Poverty and Progress in Britain, 1953–73.* Cambridge: Cambridge University Press

Fine, B. 1975. A note on 'Interpersonal comparisons and partial comparability'. *Econometrica,* 43

Floud, R. 1984. Measuring the Transformation of the European Economies. Discussion Paper no. 33. London: Centre for Economic Policy Research

Floud, R. and Wachter, K. W. 1982. Poverty and physical stature: evidence on the standard of living in London boys, 1770–1870. *Social Science History,* 6

Fogel, R. W., Engerman, S. L. and Trussell, J. 1982. Exploring the uses of data on height: the analysis of long-term trends in nutrition, labour welfare and labour productivity. *Social Science History,* 6

Foster, J. 1974. *Class Struggle and the Industrial Revolution.* London: Weidenfeld and Nicolson

Foucault, M. 1977. *Discipline and Punish: The Birth of the Prison.* London: Allen Lane

Frankel, S. H. 1953. *The Economic Impact on Underdeveloped Societies.* Oxford: Blackwell

Friedman, M. 1962. *Capitalism and Freedom.* Chicago: University of Chicago Press

Galbraith, J. K. 1974. *Economics and the Public Purpose.* London: André Deutsch

Gallais, J. 1972. Essai sur la situation actuelle des relations entre pasteurs et paysans dans le Sahel ouest-africain. *Etudes,* 36

Goodin, R. E. 1982. *Political Theory and Public Policy.* Chicago: University of Chicago Press

Goody, J. R. 1971. *Technology, Tradition and the State in Africa.* London: Oxford University Press

Gopalan, C. 1984. *Nutrition and Health Care: Problems and Policies.* New Delhi: Nutrition Foundation of India

Gorman, W. M. 1956. The demand for related goods. *Journal Paper J3129.* Ames IO: Iowa Experimental Station

Gorman, W. M. 1980 [1956]. A possible procedure for analysing quality differentials in the egg market. *Review of Economic Studies,* 47

Gosling, J. C. B. and Taylor, C. C. W. 1982. *The Greeks on Pleasure.* Oxford: Clarendon Press

Grant, J. P. 1978. *Disparity Reduction Rates in Social Indicators.* Washington DC: Overseas Development Council

Griffin, J. 1982. Modern utilitarianism. *Revue internationale de philosophie,* 36

Gugler, J. and Flanagan, W. 1978. *Urbanisation and Social Change in West Africa*. Cambridge: Cambridge University Press

Hare, R. M. 1981. *Moral Thinking: Its Level, Method and Point*. Oxford: Clarendon Press

Harsanyi, J. C. 1955. Cardinal welfare, individualistic ethics, and interpersonal comparisons of utility. *Journal of Political Economy*, 63

Hart, K. 1973. Informal income opportunities and urban enployment in Ghana. *Journal of Modern African Studies*, 11

Hart, K. 1982a. *The Political Economy of West African Agriculture*. Cambridge: Cambridge University Press

Hart, K. 1982b. On commoditisation. In *From Craft to Industry*, ed. E. Goody. Cambridge: Cambridge University Press

Hart, K. and Sperling, L. 1983. Economic categories and anthropological analysis: labour in an East African herding society. Manuscript

Hartwell, R. M. 1961. The rising standard of living in England, 1800–1850. *Economic History Review*, 14

Hartwell, R. M. and Engerman, S. 1975. Models of immiserisation: the theoretical basis of pessimism. In *The Standard of Living in Britain in the Industrial Revolution*, ed. A. J. Taylor. London: Methuen

Hartwell, R. M. and Hobsbawm, E. J. 1963. [Exchange]. *Economic History Review*, 16

Henderson, A. M. 1949. The cost of a family. *Review of Economic Studies*, 17

Henderson, W. O. 1969. *The Lancashire Cotton Famine, 1861–65*. Manchester: Manchester University Press

Henry, S. 1978. *The Hidden Economy: The Context and Control of Borderline Crime*. London: Martin Robertson

Hicks, J. R. 1971 [1942]. *The Social Framework*. Oxford: Clarendon Press

Hicks, J. R. 1981. A manifesto. In *Wealth and Welfare: Collected Essays in Economic Theory*, Vol. 1. Oxford: Blackwell

Hill, P. 1963. *Migrant Cocoa Farmers of Southern Ghana*. Cambridge: Cambridge University Press

Hirschman, A. O. 1982. *Shifting Involvements*. Princeton: Princeton University Press

Ho, T. J. 1982. *Measuring Health as a Component of Living Standards*. Living Standards Measurement Study Working Paper no. 15. Washington DC: World Bank

Hobsbawm, E. J. 1957. The British standard of living, 1790–1850. *Economic History Review*, 10

Hobsbawm, E. J. 1968. Poverty. In *Encyclopedia of the Social Sciences*. New York: Collier–Macmillan

Hollis, M. 1981. Economic man and the Original Sin. *Political Studies*, 29

Hull, C. H. 1899. *The Economic Writings of Sir William Petty*, Vol. 1. Cambridge: Cambridge University Press

James, S. 1984. *The Content of Social Explanation*. Cambridge: Cambridge University Press

Kanbur, S. M. R. 1979. Of risk taking and personal distribution of income. *Journal of Political Economy*, 91

Kapteyn, A. and Alessie, R. 1985. Habit formation and interdependent preferences in the Almost Ideal Demand System. Mimeo, Tilburg University

Kapteyn, A. and van Praag, B. 1976. A new approach to the construction of family equivalence scales. *European Economic Review*, 7

Keynes, J. M. 1936. *The General Theory of Employment, Interest and Money*. London: Macmillan

Khazanov, A. M. 1984. *Nomads and the Outside World*. Cambridge: Cambridge University Press

Kravis, I. B., Heston, A. W. and Summers, R. 1978. *International Comparisons of Real Product and Purchasing Power*. Baltimore: Johns Hopkins University Press

Kuznets, S. 1966. *Modern Economic Growth*. New Haven: Yale University Press

Kynch, J. and Sen, A. 1983. Indian women: well-being and survival. *Cambridge Journal of Economics*, 7

Lancaster, K. J. 1966. A new approach to consumer theory. *Journal of Political Economy*, 74

Luxemburg, R. 1951 [1913]. *The Accumulation of Capital*. London: Routledge and Kegan Paul

Machina, M. J. 1982. Expected utility analysis without the independence axiom. *Econometrica*, 50

Mack, J. and Lansley, S. 1985. *Poor Britain*. London: Allen and Unwin

McKeown, T. 1976. *The Modern Rise of Population*. London: Arnold

McMurrin, S. M. (ed.) 1986. *The Tanner Lectures on Human Values, VII*. Salt Lake City: University of Utah Press; Cambridge: Cambridge University Press

McNeill, W. 1976. *Plagues and Peoples*. New York: Doubleday

McPherson, M. S. 1982. Mill's moral theory and the problem of preference change. *Ethics*, 92

Majumdar, T. 1980. The rationality of changing choice. *Analyse und Kritik*, 2

Marshall, A. 1949 [1890]. *The Principles of Economics*. London: Macmillan

Marx, K. 1887. *Capital: A Critical Analysis of Capitalist Production*. London: Sonnenschein

Marx, K. and Engels, F. 1947 [1846]. *The German Ideology*. New York: International Publishers

Meade, J. E. and Stone, R. 1957 [1944]. *National Income and Expenditure*. London: Bowes and Bowes

Michael, R. and Becker, G. S. 1973. On the new theory of consumer behaviour. *Swedish Journal of Economics*, 75

Minge-Klevana, W. 1980. Does labour time decrease with industrialisation? A survey of time-allocation studies. *Current Anthropology*, 21

Morris, M. D. 1979. *Measuring the Conditions of the World's Poor: The Physical Quality of Life Index*. Oxford: Pergamon.

Muellbauer, J. 1974a. Household composition, Engel curves, and welfare comparisons between households: a duality approach. *European Economic Review*, 5

Muellbauer, J. 1974b. Household production theory, quality and the 'hedonic technique'. *American Economic Review*, 64

Muellbauer, J. 1975. Aggregation, income distribution and consumer demand. *Review of Economic Studies*, 62

Muellbauer, J. and Pashardes, P. 1982. Tests of dynamic specification and homogeneity in demand systems. Discussion paper, Birkbeck College, London

Mukerji, V. 1965. Two papers on time in economics. *Artha Vijñana*

Nagel, T. 1970. *The Possibility of Altruism*. Oxford: Clarendon Press

Nicholson, J. L. 1949. Variations in working-class family expenditure. *Journal of the Royal Statistical Society*, Series A, 112

Nussbaum, M. C. 1983–4. Plato on commensurability and desire. *Proceedings of the Aristotelian Society*, 83

Nussbaum, M. C. 1985. *Fragility of Goodness: Luck and Ethics in Greek Tragedy and Philosophy*. Cambridge: Cambridge University Press

Oakley, A. 1974. *The Sociology of Housework*. London: Martin Robertson

Pattainaik, P. K. 1980. A note on the 'rationality of becoming' and revealed preference. *Analyse und Kritik*, 2

Phlips, L. 1983 [1974]. *Applied Consumption Analysis*. Amsterdam: North-Holland

Pigou, A. C. 1952 [1920]. *The Economics of Welfare*. London: Macmillan

Polanyi, K. 1944. *The Great Transformation*. Boston: Beacon

Pollak, R. and Wachter, M. 1975. The relevance of the household production function and its implications for the allocation of time. *Journal of Political Economy*, 83

Posner, R. 1972. *Economic Analysis of Law*. Boston: Little Brown

Ramsey, F. 1926. Truth and probability. In *Foundations: Essays in Philosophy, Logic, Mathematics and Economics*. London: Routledge and Kegan Paul, 1978

Rawls, J. 1971. *A Theory of Justice*. Cambridge MA: Harvard University Press

Robbins, L. 1938. Interpersonal comparisons of utility. *Economic Journal*, 48

Rothbarth, E. 1943. Note on a method of determining equivalent income for families of different composition. In *War-Time Patterns of Saving and Spending*, ed. C. Madge. National Institute of Economic and Social Research, Occasional Paper no. 4. London: Macmillan

Sahlins, M. 1972. *Stone-Age Economics*. Chicago: Aldine

Samuelson, P. A. 1950. Evaluation of real income. *Oxford Economic Papers*, 2

Samuelson, P. A. and Swamy, S. 1974. Invariant economic index numbers and canonical duality: survey and synthesis. *American Economic Review*, 64

Schelling, T. C. 1984. Self-command in practice, in policy and in a theory of rational choice. *American Economic Review*, 74

Scitovsky, T. 1976. *The Joyless Economy*. New York: Oxford University Press

Sen, A. 1970. *Collective Choice and Social Welfare*. San Francisco: Holden Day. (Republished 1979 Amsterdam: North-Holland)

Sen, A. 1973. On the development of basic income indicators to supplement GNP measures. *ECAFE Bulletin*

Sen, A. 1974. Choice, orderings and morality. In *Practical Reason*, ed. S. Körner. Oxford: Blackwell. (Reprinted in Sen 1982)

Sen, A. 1975. The concept of efficiency in economics. In *Contemporary Issues in Economics*, ed. M. Parkin and A. R. Nobay. Manchester: Manchester University Press

Sen, A. 1976a. Poverty: an ordinal approach to measurement. *Econometrica*, 45. (Reprinted in Sen 1982)

Sen, A. 1976b. Real national income. *Review of Economic Studies*, 44. (Reprinted in Sen 1982)

Sen, A. 1977a. Rational fools: A critique of the behavioural foundations of economic theory. *Philosophy and Public Affairs*, 6. (Reprinted in Sen 1982)

Sen, A. 1977b. On weights and measures: informational constraints in social welfare analysis. *Econometrica*, 46. (Reprinted in Sen 1982)

Sen, A. 1979a. Personal utilities and public judgements: or what's wrong with welfare economics? *Economic Journal*, 89. (Reprinted in Sen 1982)

Sen, A. 1979b. Utilitarianism and welfarism. *Journal of Philosophy*, 76

Sen, A. 1980–1. Plural utility. *Proceedings of the Aristotelian Society*, 80

Sen, A. 1981. *Poverty and Famines: An Essay on Entitlement and Deprivation*. Oxford: Clarendon Press

Sen, A. 1982. *Choice, Welfare and Measurement*. Oxford: Blackwell; Cambridge MA: MIT Press

Sen, A. 1983a. Poor, relatively speaking. *Oxford Economic Papers*, 35. (Reprinted in Sen 1984a)

Sen, A. 1983b. Accounts, actions and values: objectivity of social science. In *Social Theory and Political Practice*, ed. C. Lloyd. Oxford: Clarendon Press

Sen, A. 1983c. Liberty and social choice. *Journal of Philosophy*, 80

Sen, A. 1983d. Development: Which way now? *Economic Journal*, 93. (Reprinted in Sen 1984a)

Sen, A. 1983e. Economics and the family. *Asian Development Review*, 1. (Reprinted in Sen 1984a)

Sen, A. 1984a. *Resources, Values and Development*. Cambridge MA: Harvard University Press

Sen, A. 1984b. The living standard. *Oxford Economic Papers*, 36

Sen, A. 1984c. Family and food: sex bias in poverty. In Sen 1984a

Sen, A. 1985a. *Commodities and Capabilities*. Amsterdam: North-Holland

Sen, A. 1985b. Well-being, agency and freedom. *Journal of Philosophy*, 82

Sen, A. 1985c. A reply to Professor Peter Townsend. *Oxford Economic Papers*, 37

Sen, A. and Sengupta, S. 1983. Malnutrition of rural children and the sex bias. *Economic and Political Weekly*, 19

Shackle, G. L. S. 1965. Comment on two papers on time in economics. *Artha Vijñana*

Simon, J. L. 1974. Interpersonal welfare comparisons can be made – and used for redistribution decisions. *Kyklos*, 27

Sircar, D. C. 1979. *Aśokan Studies*. Calcutta: Indian Museum

Smith, A. 1910 [1776]. *An Inquiry into the Nature and Causes of the Wealth of Nations*. London: Everyman

Spinnewyn, F. 1981. Rational habit formation. *European Economic Review*, 15

Stigler, G. J. and Becker, G. S. 1977. De gustibus non est disputandum. *American Economic Review*, 67

Stone, J. R. N. and Rowe, D. A. 1958. Dynamic demand functions: some econometric results. *Economic Journal*, 68

Streeten, P. and Burki, S. 1978. Basic needs: some issues. *World Development*, 6

Streeten, P., Burki, S., ul Haq, M., Hicks, N. and Stewart, F. 1981. *First Things First: Meeting Basic Needs in Developing Countries*. London: Oxford University Press

Studenski, P. (ed.) 1958. *The Income of Nations*. New York: New York University Press

Suppes, P. 1966. Some formal models of grading principles. *Synthese*, 6

Swift, J. 1977. Sahelian pastoralists: underdevelopment, desertification and famine. *Annual Review of Anthropology*, 6

Taylor, C. 1985. Atomism. In *Philosophy and the Human Sciences: Philosophical Papers*, Vol. 2. Cambridge: Cambridge University Press

Terleckyj, N. (ed.) 1976. *Household Production and Consumption*. New York: National Bureau of Economic Research

Thompson, E. P. 1968. *The Making of the English Working Class*. Harmondsworth: Penguin

Tilly, L. A. 1983. Food entitlement, famine and conflict. In *Hunger and History*, ed. R. I. Rotberg and T. K. Rabb. Cambridge: Cambridge University Press

Tilly, L. and Scott, J. 1978. *Women, Work and Family*. New York: Holt, Rinehart and Winston

Townsend, P. 1979a. The development of research on poverty. In Department of Health and Social Security, *Social Security Research: The Definition and Measurement of Poverty*. London: HMSO

Townsend, P. 1979b. *Poverty in the United Kingdom*. Harmondsworth: Penguin

Townsend, P. 1985. A sociological approach to the measurement of poverty: a rejoinder to Professor Amartya Sen. *Oxford Economic Papers*, 37

Tupling, G. H. 1927. *The Economic History of Rossendale*. Manchester: Manchester University Press

UNICEF 1984. *An Analysis of the Situation of Children in India*. New Delhi: UNICEF

Usher, D. 1968. *The Price Mechanism and the Meaning of National Income Statistics*. Oxford: Clarendon Press

van der Veen, R. J. 1981. Meta-rankings and collective optimality. *Social Science Information*, 20

van Herwaarden, F. G., Kapteyn, A. and van Praag, B. M. S. 1977. Twelve thousand individual welfare functions of income: a comparison of six samples in Belgium and the Netherlands. *European Economic Review*, 9

van Praag, B. M. S. 1968. *Individual Welfare Functions and Consumer Behaviour*. Amsterdam: North-Holland

van Praag, B. M. S., Hagenaars, A. J. M. and van Weeren, H. 1982. Poverty in Europe. *Journal of Income and Wealth*, 28

Vickrey, W. 1945. Measuring marginal utility by reactions to risk. *Econometrica*, 13

von Tunzelmann, N. 1985. The standard of living debate and optimal economic growth. In *The Economics of the Industrial Revolution*, ed. J. Mokyr. London: Allen and Unwin

Weber, M., ed. Roth, G. and Wittich, C. 1978. *Economy and Society*. Berkeley and Los Angeles: University of California Press

Weber, M. 1981 [1923]. *General Economic History*. New Brunswick: Transaction

Wedderburn, D. (ed.) 1974. *Poverty, Inequality and the Class Structure*. Cambridge: Cambridge University Press

Wells, J. 1983. Industrial accumulation and living standards in the long-run: the São Paulo industrial working class, 1930–75. *Journal of Development Studies*, 19

Williams, B. 1973. A critique of utilitarianism. In J. J. C. Smart and B. Williams, *Utilitarianism: For and Against*. Cambridge: Cambridge University Press

Williams, B. 1981. Moral luck. In *Moral Luck and Other Essays*. Cambridge: Cambridge University Press

Williams, B. 1985. *Ethics and the Limits of Philosophy*. Cambridge MA: Harvard University Press; London: Fontana

Winston, G. C. 1980. Addiction and backsliding: a theory of compulsive consumption. *Journal of Economic Behaviour and Organisation*, 1

World Bank 1983. *World Development Report 1983*. New York: Oxford University Press

World Bank 1984. *World Development Report 1984*. New York: Oxford University Press

Yaari, M. E. and Bar-Hillel, M. 1984. On dividing justly. *Social Choice and Welfare*, 1

Index